STIR FRY RECIPES

A Vegetable Stir Fry Cookbook for Effortless Meals

(Quick Easy and Tasty Stir Fry Recipes for Your Everyday Meals)

Ashley Welter

Published by Sharon Lohan

© Ashley Welter

All Rights Reserved

Stir Fry Recipes: A Vegetable Stir Fry Cookbook for Effortless Meals (Quick Easy and Tasty Stir Fry Recipes for Your Everyday Meals)

ISBN 978-1-990334-48-1

All rights reserved. No part of this guide may be reproduced in any form without permission in writing from the publisher except in the case of brief quotations embodied in critical articles or reviews.

Legal & Disclaimer

The information contained in this book is not designed to replace or take the place of any form of medicine or professional medical advice. The information in this book has been provided for educational and entertainment purposes only.

The information contained in this book has been compiled from sources deemed reliable, and it is accurate to the best of the Author's knowledge; however, the Author cannot guarantee its accuracy and validity and cannot be held liable for any errors or omissions. Changes are periodically made to this book. You must consult your doctor or get professional medical advice before using any of the suggested remedies, techniques, or information in this book.

Table of contents

Part 1 1
Introduction 2
Stir-Fry Recipes 5
Stir-Fry Recipes 5
Stir-Fried Vegetables with Peanut Butter 5
Collard Green Stir-Fry With Almonds 7
Asparagus Stir-Fry In Teriyaki Sauce 8
Squash, Zucchini And Carrot Stir-Fry 9
Stir-Fried Green Onion And Eggs 10
Brussels Sprouts And Potato Stir-Fry 11
Stir-Fried Asparagus With Ginger And Sesame Seeds 12
Stir-Fried Broccoli And Shrimp In Coconut Milk 14
Shrimp And Mushroom Stir-Fry In Sesame Oil And Oyster Sauce 16
Stir-Fried Beef Sirloin With Shiitake Mushrooms 18
Stir-Fried Spicy Orange Beef 20
Black Peppered Stir-Fried Beef 22
Stir-Fried Ribeye In Rice Vinegar 23
Stir-Fried Chicken with Eggplant and Spinach 25
Stir-Fried Chicken and Vegetables with Pecans 27
Honey Chicken Stir-Fry With Cashews 28
Lemon Pork Stir-Fry With Cilantro 30
Stir-Fried Sake Pork 32
Stir-Fried Peppered Pork With Onions 33

Pork Stir-Fry In Hoisin Sauce 34
Stir Fry Recipes 35
36. Asparagus, Yellow Squash, And Cod 35
37. Thai Green Prawn Curry 38
38. Prawn And Vegetable Omelet 41
39. Scallops And Asparagus 44
40. Squid With Thai Basil 46
41. Cucumber And Vietnamese Seafood 48
42. Seafood With Fried Rice 51
43. Garlic Seafood Marinara 54
44. Chinese Fish Fillets 56
Vegetables Stir-Fry Recipes 59
45. Pak Choy/Bok Choy 59
46. Lo Mein With Charred Cabbage, Shiitake, And Chives 61
47. Smacked Cucumber 64
48. Hoisin-Glazed Tofu (Bean Curd) And Brown Rice 66
49. Aubergine (Eggplant) And Sesame Seeds 68
50. Stir-Fry Vegetables 70
51. Sesame Vegetables With Rice 72
52. Garbanzo 74
53. Broccoli Noodles And Spicy Mushroom 76
54. Seitan (Wheat Gluten) And Black Bean 78
55. Gingered Tofu, Pea Noodles And Aubergine (Eggplant) .. 81
Part 2 83
Introduction 84
Velvet Chicken & Cashew Nut Stir Fry 85
Spicy Salmon Stir Fry 87

Stir Fried Teriyaki Tofu	89
Ginger & Lime Infused King Prawn Stir Fry	91
Healthy Quinoa Stir Fry	93
Smoked Salmon & Bean Sprout Stir Fry	95
Mushroom & Ostrich Stir Fry	97
Exotic Mango And Mushroom Stir Fry	98
Chicken And Fig Stir Fry	99
Thai Red Curry Stir Fry	101
Chicken Stir Fry With Hoi Sin Sauce	103
Delicious Coconut Pork	104
Prawn And Pineapple On Coconut Rice	106
Healthy Beef Stir Fry	108
Vegetarian Apple-Cinnamon And Brussel Sprout Stir Fry	110
Superfood Stir Fry	112
Delicious Mussel Stir Fry	113
Nutty Stir Fry	114
Mediterranean Style Stir Fry	115
Octopus Stir Fry	117
Vegan Stir Fry	119
Colorful Stir Fry With Bamboo Shoots	120
Coconut, Feta & Spinach Stir Fry	122
Spicy Beef Noodles	123
Stir Fry Recipes	125
1) Stir Fry With Ground Beef	125
2) Stir Fry With Chinese Sausage	127
3) Stir Fry With Bean Sprout	129
4) Stir Fry With Lemon And Butter	130

5) Stir Fry With Oyster Sauce...131
6) Stir Fry With Duck..133
7) Stir Fry With Peanuts..135
8) Stir Fry With Salmon...137
9) Stir Fry With Crab Meat...139
10) Stir Fry With Walnuts..140
11) Stir Fry With Grilled Chicken...142
12) Stir Fry With Ground Pork..144
13) Stir Fry With Bacon..146
14) Stir Fry With Chicken Hotdog...148
15) Stir Fry With Shredded Meat..150
16) Stir Fry With Tomato Sauce 152
17) Stir Fry With Cauliflower..154
18) Stir Fry With Mushrooms And Carrots 155
19) Stir Fry With Cabbage 157
20)   Stir Fry With Raisins..159
21) Stir Fry With Corn..161
22)   Stir Fry With Capsicum 162
23)   Stir Fry With Fried Cashews..163
24)   Stir Fry With Coriander Seed And Mango..............................165
25)   Stir Fry With Apricots..167
26)   Plain Stir Fry...169
27)   Stir Fry With Shallots...170
28)   Stir Fry With Ginger...171
29)   Stir Fry With Broccoli...172
30)   Stir Fry With Mozzarella Cheese And Ketchup......................174
31) Stir Fry With Cherry Tomatoes 176

Cauliflower Chicken Fried Rice 178

Cheesy Chicken Stir Fry 180

Chef John's Caramel Chicken 182

Chef John's Cashew Chicken 183

Chettinad Style Chicken 185

Chicken 'n' Peppers 187

Chicken Apricot Stir Fry 188

Chicken Broccoli Ca Unieng's Style .... **Error! Bookmark not defined.**

Part 1

Introduction

Stir-fry is probably one of the most flexible meals that you can easily make. You can choose the ingredients that you want to eat and simply combine them. You can mix meat with vegetables, fish with chicken or whatever combination that you can think of. Making stir-fried meals is easy, but here are a few tips to make sure that your stir-fried dishes are perfect.

- You don't have to have a wok to make stir-fried meals. You can simply use a large skillet or a flat-bottomed pan which is big enough to accommodate all the ingredients that you want to combine. Also, you have to make sure that all of your ingredients can make contact with the heated surface.
- Heat settings may vary from person to person. However, it is best to set the temperature at medium-high so that you have a reasonable amount of time to cook and stir-fry without worrying about burning the ingredients.

- Make sure to allow the oil to heat up before cooking your ingredients in it. If you are not using any type of cooking oil, allow the pan to thoroughly heat up as well.
- Make sure to prepare the ingredients before you start cooking. Chop the vegetables, slice your meat, and arrange them in the order you want to cook them. This is especially important because making stir-fried meals requires you to be quick. Preparing your ingredients and knowing which ones you'd put in the wok or skillet next will avoid burning and overcooked food.
- It is best to chop and slice the ingredients the same size so that they'd take more or less the same time to cook. If you want a certain ingredient to be bigger than your other ingredients, it is advisable that you cook them first and then simply put it back in the wok or skillet to reheat it a few minutes before you finish cooking.
- If you are cooking with meat such as beef and pork or chicken and fish, you should cook them first until they are slightly cooked and set them aside. Then, continue cooking the rest of the ingredients such as vegetables and fruits. As mentioned earlier, you can simply put the meat back in the skillet for reheating before you are finished cooking.
- Always cook bigger and thicker vegetables first because they take longer. For example, cook the carrots and broccoli first until they start to become soft and then add the tomatoes, onions and garlic.

- To make a stir-fried meal delicious, you always have to keep it moving. Stirring constantly will distribute the flavors evenly and if using sauces, coat your ingredients evenly.
- Since ingredients in a stir-fried dish are cut and sliced into small pieces, it is best to serve it immediately as it only takes a while for the ingredients to cool down.
- The best thing about stir-fried dishes is they can be served with or without rice. If you feel like having or serving them with rice, then you can simply put your stir-fried vegetables or meat on top but if you don't, you can eat or serve them alone and they will still taste delicious.

Stir-Fry Recipes

Stir-Fry Recipes

Stir-Fried Vegetables with Peanut Butter

Prep Time: **5 minutes**
Servings: **6**

Ingredients:

2 tablespoons of soy sauce
1 tablespoon of brown sugar
2 teaspoons of garlic powder
2 teaspoons of peanut butter
2 teaspoons of olive oil
1 16-ounce package of frozen mixed vegetables

Directions:

1. In a small bowl, whisk together soy sauce, brown sugar, garlic powder and peanut butter.
2. Heat olive oil in a large skillet or wok over medium heat. Add the frozen vegetables and cook and stir for 5-7 minutes or until tender.
3. Transfer vegetables to a serving dish and pour soy sauce mixture all over.
4. Serve.

Collard Green Stir-Fry With Almonds

Prep Time: **10 minutes**
Servings: **2**

Ingredients:

2 cup of water
1 cup of cooked white rice
1 tablespoon of sesame oil
5 cups of chopped collard greens
1/8 teaspoon of minced garlic
1 pinch of red pepper flakes
1/3 cup of almonds
1 teaspoon of lemon juice
1 teaspoon of soy sauce
¼ teaspoon of chopped fresh ginger

Directions:

1. Heat sesame oil in a large skillet or wok over medium heat. Add the collard greens, garlic and red pepper flakes and cook and stir for 10 minutes or until tender and wilted
2. Toss in the almonds and stir in lemon juice, soy sauce and ginger.
3. Simmer for 5 minutes or until liquid evaporates.
4. Transfer to a serving dish and serve with the rice.

Asparagus Stir-Fry In Teriyaki Sauce

Prep Time: **10 minutes**
Servings: **4**

Ingredients:

1 tablespoon of butter
¼ sweet onion, chopped
1 pound of fresh asparagus, trimmed
1 teaspoon of chopped, roasted garlic
2 teaspoons of teriyaki sauce

Directions:

1. Melt in a large skillet over medium heat. Sauté the onions until translucent and tender. Add the asparagus and cook and stir for 3-5 minutes or until heated through.
2. Transfer asparagus to a serving dish and pour teriyaki sauce all over.
3. Serve.

Squash, Zucchini And Carrot Stir-Fry

Prep Time: **10 minutes**
Servings: **6**

Ingredients:

1 tablespoon of olive oil
2 medium yellow squash, sliced
2 medium zucchini, sliced
½ 16-ounce package of baby-cut carrots
1 medium red onion, cut in half and sliced
2 packets of concentrated vegetable broth

Directions:

1. Heat olive oil in a large skillet or wok over medium heat. Add squash, zucchini, carrots and onions and cook and stir for 5-7 minutes or until tender but crisp.
2. Stir in broth and stir for 2 minutes.
3. Transfer vegetables to a serving dish and serve.

Stir-Fried Green Onion And Eggs

Prep Time: **5 minutes**
Servings: **4**

Ingredients:

2 tablespoons of vegetable oil
6 eggs, beaten
1 green onion, chopped
2 large tomatoes, cut into wedges
Salt to taste

Directions:

1. Heat olive oil in a large skillet over medium heat. Add the eggs and green onion and cook and stir for 3 minutes or until egg is cooked and solid.
2. Add the tomatoes and stir-fry until firm.
3. Season with salt.
4. Transfer to a serving dish.
5. Serve.

Brussels Sprouts And Potato Stir-Fry

Prep Time: **15 minutes**
Servings: **8**

Ingredients:

1 tablespoon of vegetable oil
1 onion, chopped
1 large potato, peeled and cubed
1 bay leaf
1 pound of Brussels sprouts, trimmed and cut lengthwise
1 red pepper, seeded and cut into ½-inch cubes
¼ cup of chicken broth
Black pepper to taste
2 tablespoon of chopped green onions

Directions:

1. Heat olive oil in a large skillet over medium heat. Add the onion, potato and bay leaf and cook and stir for 5 minutes or until onion is translucent.
2. Add the Brussels sprouts, red pepper and chicken broth. Cover skillet and let vegetables cook for 10 minutes or until tender.
3. Season with black pepper.
4. Transfer to a serving dish and sprinkle green onions on top.
5. Serve.

Stir-Fried Asparagus With Ginger And Sesame Seeds

Prep Time: **10 minutes**
Servings: **6**

Ingredients:

2 pounds of asparagus, cut into 1-inch pieces
2 teaspoons of sesame seeds
2 tablespoons of peanut oil
2 teaspoons of grated fresh ginger
½ teaspoon of salt
1 teaspoon of sesame oil
Dash of salt

Directions:

1. Fill a pot with water and sprinkle with a dash of salt. Bring to a boil and add the asparagus. Cook for 2-3 minutes. Remove asparagus from the boiling water and immediately plunge into ice water.
2. Pat dry asparagus with paper towels.
3. Heat a skillet over medium heat and toast the sesame seeds for 3-5 minutes or until lightly browned. Transfer to a dish and set aside.

4. Heat peanut oil in a large skillet over medium heat. Add the ginger and asparagus and cook and stir for 5 minutes or until ginger is fragrant.
5. Season with salt.
6. Transfer to a serving dish. Drizzle sesame oil all over and sprinkle toasted sesame seeds on top.
7. Serve.

Stir-Fried Broccoli And Shrimp In Coconut Milk

Prep Time: **15 minutes**
Servings: **4**

Ingredients:

1 ½ cups of coconut milk
1 tablespoon of minced ginger
1 tablespoon of lime juice
1 tablespoon of fish sauce
1 teaspoon of oyster sauce
2 teaspoons of minced garlic
½ teaspoon of chili garlic sauce
2 tablespoons of white sugar
1 tablespoon of avocado oil
1 pound of medium-sized shrimp, peeled and deveined
½ onion, sliced
1 ½ teaspoons of curry powder
2 cups of broccoli florets

Directions:

1. In a small bowl, mix together coconut milk, ginger, lime juice, fish sauce, oyster sauce, minced garlic, chili garlic sauce and white sugar.
2. Heat avocado oil in a wok or a large skillet over medium heat. Stir-fry shrimp until pink, 3-5 minutes. Remove shrimp from the skillet and set aside.

3. Add onion and curry powder to the skillet. Cook for 2 minutes and then stir in the broccoli. Stir-fry for 3 minutes more. Add the coconut milk mixture to the skillet and bring to a boil. Reduce the heat and simmer for 3 minutes.
4. Place shrimp back in the skillet and stir for 3 minutes or until shrimp is heated through.
5. Transfer to a dish.
6. Serve.

Shrimp And Mushroom Stir-Fry In Sesame Oil And Oyster Sauce

Prep Time: **20 minutes**
Servings: **4**

Ingredients:

1 tablespoon of sesame oil
1 tablespoon of olive oil
1 pound of tiger shrimp, peeled and deveined
1 cup of chopped onion
1 ½ cups of sliced king mushrooms
½ cup of chopped green bell pepper
3 garlic cloves, finely chopped
1 teaspoon of fresh minced ginger
½ cup of water
1 teaspoon of oyster sauce
2 cups of bean sprouts

Directions:

1. Heat both sesame and olive oil in a wok or in a large skillet over medium heat. Stir in shrimp and onion and cook until well coated. Stir in mushrooms, green bell pepper and garlic cloves. Add in the ginger and stir.

2. Pour oyster sauce and water into the skillet and simmer for 5 minutes or until shrimp turns bright pink.
3. Add the bean sprouts to the skillet and toss to combine.
4. Cook for 2 minutes more and transfer to a dish.
5. Serve.

Stir-Fried Beef Sirloin With Shiitake Mushrooms

Prep Time: 20 minutes
Servings: **8**

Ingredients:

2 pounds of boneless beef sirloin
3 tablespoons of cornstarch
1 10.5-ounce can of beef broth
½ cup of soy sauce
2 tablespoons of sugar
2 tablespoons of vegetable oil
4 cups of sliced shitake mushrooms
1 head of Chinese cabbage, thinly sliced
2 medium red peppers, cut into strips
3 celery stalks, sliced
2 medium green onions, cut into 2-inch pieces
8 cups of cooked white rice

Directions:

1. Slice the beef sirloin into very thin strips.
2. In a bowl, combine cornstarch, beef broth, soy sauce and sugar. Mix well.
3. Heat 1 tablespoon of vegetable oil in a large skillet or wok and add the beef. Stir-fry for 5-7 minutes or

until browned. Remove the beef from the skillet and set aside.
4. Add the remaining olive oil in the skillet and add the mushrooms, cabbage, red peppers, celery stalks and green onions. Stir-fry for 5-7 minutes or until tender but crisp. Remove from the skillet and set aside.
5. Add the cornstarch mixture and bring to a boil, stirring constantly. Put back beef and vegetables in the skillet and cook for 2 minutes or just until heated through.
6. Evenly divide stir-fried beef into 8 and place on individual plates. Serve with rice.

Stir-Fried Spicy Orange Beef

Prep Time: **15 minutes**
Servings: **4**

Ingredients:

¼ cup of vegetable oil
¼ cup of cornstarch
1 16-ounce package of firm tofu, drained and cut into strips
2 tablespoons of soy sauce
½ cup of orange juice
¼ cup of warm water
1 tablespoon of sugar
1 teaspoon of chili paste
1 teaspoon of cornstarch
1 tablespoon of vegetable oil
2 carrots, sliced

Directions:

1. Heat ¼ cup of vegetable oil in a large skillet over medium heat.
2. Place ¼ cup of cornstarch in a shallow bowl and press tofu on the cornstarch. Make sure to coat all sides.
3. Place tofu in the skillet and stir-fry for 5 minutes or until golden brown on all sides.

4. Remove tofu from the skillet and place in a paper-lined plate.
5. Mix together soy sauce, orange juice, water, sugar, chili paste and the remaining cornstarch in a bowl.
6. Heat the remaining vegetable oil in the skillet and stir-fry the carrots for 5 minutes or until tender. Add the soy sauce mixture to the skillet and bring to a boil.
7. Return tofu to the skillet and stir-fry for 3 minutes more or until evenly coated with the sauce.
8. Transfer to a dish.
9. Serve.

Black Peppered Stir-Fried Beef

Prep Time: **15 minutes**
Servings: **4**

Ingredients:

2 tablespoons of vegetable oil
4 garlic cloves, chopped
½ pound of ground beef
½ small head of cabbage, shredded
1 red bell pepper, cut into strips
2 tablespoons of soy sauce
1 teaspoon of cornstarch
½ cup of water
1 teaspoon of ground black pepper

Directions:

1. Heat vegetable oil in a large skillet over medium heat. Add the garlic and sauté for 5 minutes. Add ground beef and stir-fry until beef has turned brown. Add the cabbage and pepper and cook until vegetables are tender and beef is thoroughly cooked.
2. Stir in soy sauce. In a bowl, mix together cornstarch and water until smooth and add to the skillet.
3. Season with pepper and continue cooking until sauce has thickened.
4. Transfer to a serving dish.

5. Serve.

Stir-Fried Ribeye In Rice Vinegar

Prep Time: **20 minutes**
Servings: **4**

Ingredients:

¾ boneless rib eye
1 tablespoon of cornstarch
3 tablespoons of Kikkoman soy sauce
1 garlic clove, minced
½ teaspoon of sugar
1 pound of fresh broccoli, trimmed
4 teaspoons of cornstarch
½ teaspoon of crushed red pepper
3 tablespoons of vegetable oil
1 medium onion, thinly sliced
2 teaspoons of seasoned rice vinegar

Directions:

1. Slice the beef across the grain into thin slices.
2. In a bowl, mix together 1 tablespoon of cornstarch, 1 tablespoon of soy sauce, garlic and sugar. Add the beef and marinate for 10 minutes.
3. Cut broccoli into bite size pieces

4. Mix together 1 cup of water, 2 tablespoons of soy sauce, 4 teaspoons of cornstarch and crushed red pepper in a bowl. Set aside.
5. Heat 1 tablespoon of vegetable oil in a work or in a large skillet. Add the beef and stir-fry for 3 minutes. Remove from the skillet and set aside.
6. Heat the remaining 2 tablespoons of vegetable in the skillet. Add the broccoli and onion and sauté for 2 minutes. Pour tablespoon of water over the vegetables. Cover the skillet and cook for 2 minutes. Make sure to stir occasionally.
7. Return beef to the skillet and pour the soy sauce mixture. Cook until sauce starts to boil and thicken.
8. Transfer to a dish and serve.

Stir-Fried Chicken with Eggplant and Spinach

Prep Time: **20 minutes**
Servings: **4**

Ingredients:

½ large eggplant, sliced into rounds
1/8 teaspoon of salt
4 skinless, boneless chicken breasts, cut into cubes
2 garlic cloves, minced
2 tablespoons of soy sauce
1 tablespoon of canola oil
2 cups of sliced mushrooms
1/8 teaspoon of ground black pepper
4 cups of spinach

Directions:

1. Season eggplant with salt. Leave for 5 minutes and then cut into cubes.
2. Heat a skillet over medium heat and add the chicken, garlic and soy sauce. Cook for 5-7 minutes or until chicken is thoroughly cooked.
3. Stir in mushrooms and season with black pepper. Stir-fry for 2-3 minutes or until mushrooms are browned.
4. In a separate skillet, heat canola oil and add the eggplant. Cook until lightly browned. Place cooked eggplant in the skillet with the chicken.

5. Add spinach to the skillet with the chicken and eggplant and cook until soft and wilted, 2-3 minutes.
6. Transfer to a dish and serve.

Stir-Fried Chicken and Vegetables with Pecans

Prep Time: **15 minutes**
Servings: **4**

Ingredients:

1 tablespoon of extra virgin olive oil
4 skinless, boneless chicken breasts, cut into strips
1 cup of julienned carrots
1 small onion, chopped
1 cup of fresh sliced mushrooms
1 zucchini squash, peeled cut into rounds
2 yellow summer squash, peeled and cut into chunks
½ cup of pecans
1 teaspoon of ground black pepper

Directions:

1. Heat olive oil in a large skillet over medium heat. Add the chicken and stir-fry until lightly brown. Stir in carrots and onion and cook for 3 minutes.
2. Add the mushrooms, zucchini and squash. Stir-fry until squash starts to soften. Stir in the pecans and season with pepper.
3. Stir-fry for 2-3 minutes.
4. Transfer to a serving dish.
5. Serve.

Honey Chicken Stir-Fry With Cashews

Prep Time: **10 minutes**
Servings: **6**

Ingredients:

2 teaspoons of peanut oil
2 celery stalks, chopped
2 carrots, peeled and sliced lengthwise
1 ½ pounds of skinless, boneless, chicken breasts, cut into strips
1 tablespoon of cornstarch
¾ cup of orange juice
3 tablespoons of light soy sauce
1 tablespoon of honey
1 teaspoon of minced fresh ginger root
¼ cup of cashews
¼ cup of minced green onions

Directions:

1. Heat 1 teaspoon of peanut oil in a large skillet over medium heat. Add the carrots and celery and cook for 3 minutes.
2. Add the remaining peanut oil. Add the chicken and stir-fry for 5minutes more.
3. Combine cornstarch and orange juice in a small bowl. Mix until cornstarch is dissolved. Stir in soy sauce, honey and ginger. Pour sauce into the skillet

and cook until sauce has thickened, stirring occasionally.
4. Transfer to a serving dish and sprinkle cashews and green onions on top.
5. Serve.

Lemon Pork Stir-Fry With Cilantro

Prep Time: **25 minutes**
Servings: **4**

Ingredients:

¼ cup of olive oil
½ cup of finely chopped fresh cilantro leaves
1 tablespoon of finely chopped fresh ginger
4 garlic cloves, finely chopped
1 pound of pork tenderloin, thinly sliced
2 tablespoons of olive oil, divided
2 onions, thinly sliced
1 red bell pepper, thinly sliced
1 tablespoon of lime juice
½ cup of chopped fresh cilantro

Directions:

1. In a large bowl, mix together olive oil, cilantro, ginger and garlic. Add the pork and toss well to coat. Cover the bowl with cling wrap and place in the refrigerator overnight or for at least 8 hours.
2. Heat 1 tablespoon of olive oil in a large skillet. Remove pork from the marinade and place in the skillet. Stir-fry for 10 minutes or until browned. Remove from the skillet and set aside.
3. Add the remaining olive oil to the skillet and add the onions. Cook for 3 minutes or until translucent. Add

the red bell pepper and cook for 3 minutes more. Return pork to the skillet. Stir in lime juice and cilantro. Stir-fry for 1 minute or until cilantro has wilted.
4. Transfer to a dish and serve.

Stir-Fried Sake Pork

Prep Time: **10 minutes**
Servings: **4**

Ingredients:

1 tablespoon of grated fresh ginger root
2 tablespoons of soy sauce
2 tablespoons of sake
2 tablespoons of mirin
1 pound of thinly sliced pork loin
3 tablespoons of vegetable oil

Directions:

1. Whisk together ginger, soy sauce, sake and mirin in a bowl. Add the pork and marinade for 1 hour.
2. Heat the oil in a skillet and add the pork. Stir-fry until browned and slightly crispy.
3. Transfer to a dish and serve.

Stir-Fried Peppered Pork With Onions

Prep Time: **10 minutes**
Servings: **6**

Ingredients:

2 tablespoons of vegetable oil
2 pounds of pork loin, thinly sliced
1 teaspoon of salt
2 tablespoons of butter
1 onion, thinly sliced
2 teaspoons of ground black pepper

Directions:

1. Heat vegetable oil in a large skillet. Add the pork and season with salt. Cook for 5-10 minutes or until browned. Remove from the skillet and set aside.
2. Melt the butter in the same skillet. Add the onions and sauté for 5 minutes. Return pork to the skillet and sprinkle with black pepper.
3. Stir-fry for 5 minutes or until heated through.
4. Transfer to a dish and serve.

Pork Stir-Fry In Hoisin Sauce

Prep Time: **25 minutes**
Servings: **4**

Ingredients:

1 pound of boneless pork chops, cut into strips
3 tablespoons of hoisin sauce
½ onion, sliced
1 tablespoon of cornstarch
1 teaspoon of red pepper flakes
1 tablespoon of sesame oil

Directions:

1. Mix 1 tablespoon of hoisin sauce and cornstarch in a bowl.
2. Heat the sesame oil in a skillet over medium heat and add the pork and onion. Stir-fry for 5 minutes or until pork has browned and onion has turned translucent.
3. Stir in the remaining 2 tablespoons of hoisin sauce and continue cooking for 3 minutes or until pork is thoroughly coated with the sauce.
4. Transfer to a dish and serve.

Stir Fry Recipes

36. Asparagus, Yellow Squash, And Cod

The cod is water-velveted to tenderize the meat. It is a light and delicate meal with vegetables making it a perfect dish while balancing the nutrients.

Cooking time: 45 minutes
Serving: 2

Ingredients

Cod ingredients

- Cod (or halibut – a white fish), ¼-inch slices – ½ pound
- Cornstarch – 2 teaspoons
- Lightly beaten egg white – 1 tablespoon
- Sake or Chinese rice wine- 2 teaspoons
- Kosher salt – ¼ teaspoon

- Vegetable or canola oil – 1 teaspoon
- Water – 6 cups

Stir fry ingredients

- Finely minced medium garlic clove – 1
- Low-sodium chicken stock, bought or homemade – 3 tablespoons
- Sesame oil – 1 teaspoon
- Vegetable or canola oil – 1 tablespoon
- Cornstarch – 1 teaspoon
- Yellow squash (from summer), 1/8-inch slices – ¼ pound
- Kosher salt to taste
- Garden asparagus (sparrow grass), trim ends, cut into ½-inch lengths – ¼ pound
- White rice, cooked and ready to serve

Directions

Preparing the cod

1. Take a small bowl and thoroughly mix the following: cornstarch, egg white, salt and rice wine. Put the cod in another bowl and pour the mixture you prepared in step 1 on it. Toss gently to coat the cod.
2. Once the cod is coated, refrigerate it for thirty minutes. After the sitting time, put water in a wok and bring to boil. Add oil at boiling point. After the oil, proceed to add the cod.

3. Cook and stir with a strainer or chopsticks until the outer surface is opaque but raw inside. It should take you 30 seconds.
4. When the cod becomes opaque, use a colander (bowl-shaped strainer) to remove the cod, shaking the excess water. When the wok is empty, clean the wok to dry.

Stir-fry preparation

1. Take a small bowl and mix the following: garlic, chicken stock cornstarch and sesame oil. After mixing, take the wok, this time clean and put the vegetable oil before heating until it smokes. Follow by adding asparagus and squash and proceed to cook and stir for 30 seconds.
2. Add the cod you prepared and cook as you gently stir. Continue stirring in the same manner for a minute to avoid breaking it up.
3. Once the minute is over, put sauce in the wok and season with salt. Cook and keep stirring gently until the fish and vegetables get coated and the sauce thickens. Once you get a thick sauce, remove the wok from the heat and serve with the cooked white rice.

37. Thai Green Prawn Curry

You can substitute the prawn with chicken in this recipe.

Cooking time: 35 minutes
Serving: 4

Ingredients

Paste ingredients

- Ground coriander – 1 ½ teaspoons
- Ground cumin seeds – ½ teaspoon
- Minced ginger root – 3 teaspoons
- Green chilies – 2-3
- Minced garlic cloves – 4 teaspoons
- Fresh coriander, chopped – 6 full tablespoons
- Lemongrass (or 1 ½ lemon to make lemon zest) – 3 stalks
- Lime zest – make from 1 lime

- Lime juice – squeeze 2 limes
- Frying oil – 2 tablespoons

Other ingredients

- Tiger prawns (raw or cooked), peel and remove dorsal vein – 300 grams (¾ pounds)
- Mangetout or green beans – 200 grams (½ pound)
- Frying oil – 4 tablespoons
- Coconut milk – 400ml
- Baby corn – 200 grams (½ pound)
- Soy sauce – 3 tablespoons

Directions

1. Start by doing either of the following: Put the ingredients from the paste section in a food processor to form a thick paste, smooth in nature or, chop all the ingredients (still in the same part) finely and mix thoroughly.
2. After mixing, heat a wok and then proceed to add oil. After the oil, put baby corn and beans and stir-fry for 40 seconds. Add the paste you made in step 1 together with coconut milk and let them boil lightly.
3. After the light boiling, switch the heat to medium so that the paste can simmer for 5-7 minutes.
4. After the 6th-7th minute, put the prawns in the wok then cook and stir for 3-5 minutes. If the sauce is

too thick, you can add some water. On the other hand, if it is thin, reduce the heat again.
5. After five minutes are over, remove the wok from heat and serve immediately. Best served with jasmine rice.

38. Prawn And Vegetable Omelet

Colorful vegetables with a layer of omelet add taste to the prawn.

Cooking time: 30 minutes
Serving: 4

Ingredients

- Raw prawns, peel, thawed (unfreeze) and drained – 350 grams (0.8 pounds)
- Toasted sesame oil – 1 teaspoon
- Eggs – 8
- Fresh and chopped coriander – 3 tablespoons (optional)
- Light soy sauce – 1 tablespoon
- Corn flour – 2 teaspoons
- Sherry wine (medium or dry) – 2 tablespoons
- Broccoli florets, cut to thin slices – 300 grams (¾ pounds)
- Vegetable oil – 2 tablespoons

- Red or orange pepper, seeded and thinly sliced – 3
- Chopped garlic cloves – 2
- Fresh ginger root, peeled and cut into thin strips – 50 grams (2 teaspoons)
- Sliced spring onions – 4
- Bean sprouts (from germinating bean seeds) – 200 grams (½ pound)

Directions

1. In one bowl, beat the eggs together with sesame oil and coriander, if available and set aside. Proceed to take another bowl and mix corn flour, sherry, and soy sauce to form a smooth paste and set aside too.
2. Now, it's time to cook after the first two steps. In a large wok/ non-stick frying pan, heat half of the vegetable oil. Once the oil is heated, add pepper, broccoli, garlic, ginger and spring onions. After the addition, cook as you stir for about 5 minutes until the broccoli looks tender and bright green.
3. Next, pour the soy sauce mixture you prepared in step 2 to the wok and stir for a minute. Follow by adding prawns and cook for another 2 minutes. Follow by adding bean sprouts and slightly stir for one minute. The prawn should turn pink before going to the next step.
4. After the oink turn, transfer the prawn to a large bowl and cover to keep it warm. Is the wok empty? Wipe it using a kitchen paper. Once it's clean, pour the remaining oil and heat for a few seconds.

5. Slowly, put over half of the egg mixture and spread evenly using circular motions. Stir the egg once or twice and let it cook and settle for three minutes. After the third minute, slice out the omelet to loosen it and put the pieces in a serving dish.
6. Add the remaining egg mixture quickly and cook for 1-2 minutes until it appears just set. When the egg is ready, put it on a board and cut into ribbons.
7. Next, go back to the omelet you earlier set aside and sprinkle the vegetables with a spoon. Finally, sprinkle the omelet ribbons on top before serving.

39. Scallops And Asparagus

Cooking time: 30 minutes
Serving: 4

Ingredients

- Scallops, thawed (unfreeze) if frozen – 5-8 large ones
- Frying oil – 1 teaspoon and one tablespoon, separate
- Asparagus, trimmed and chopped into 3 cm pieces – 15 spears (pieces)
- Salt and pepper – as preferred
- Corn flour – as preferred
- Garlic, chopped – 1 tablespoon
- Medium onion, chopped – 1
- Finely chopped shallot – 1
- Water – 125ml (about a cup)
- Salt to taste

- Chicken stock granules (bought) – 1 teaspoon (or two teaspoons of chicken broth)
- Corn flour mixed with water – 1 teaspoon and two teaspoons respectively
- Red pepper, cut into cubes – ½
- Sesame oil – 1 teaspoon

Directions

1. Start by briefly cooking the asparagus in boiling water for three minutes together with a teaspoon of oil. After the third minute, set it aside.
2. Next, put the scallops in a bowl and season them with salt and pepper. After seasoning, cover them lightly with corn flour. After preparing the scallops, heat a tablespoon of oil over high heat.
3. When the pan is hot, put the shallot and garlic. Stir-fry them for 2-3 minutes until fragrance. At this point, add onions and salt and proceed to cook for 3-4 minutes until the onions go soft. Put the scallops and stir-fry for another 3-4 minutes until both sides have an even brown color.
4. After the scallops go brown, switch the heat to medium and add chicken stock granules (or chicken broth) then let everything to simmer for 2 minutes. Next, put red pepper in and stir. Follow by switching the heat back to high.
5. Once the heat is at high level, add the cornflour mixture, asparagus, sesame oil, and salt. Stir as the

sauce heats through until it is slightly thick. When it's ready, remove the pan from heat and serve.

40. Squid With Thai Basil

You can substitute with local basil. Serve the squid during lunch or dinner with white rice.

Cooking time: 45 minutes
Serving: 4

Ingredients

- Squid tubes, halved, mark with knife cuts (score) and cut to bite size – 2
- Corn flour – as preferred
- Salt and pepper
- Frying oil – 2 tablespoons and one tablespoon separated
- Chopped spring onions – 2
- Chopped garlic – 2 teaspoons

- Shallot, cut into dices – 1
- Salt – ½ teaspoon
- Chopped onion – 1 medium size
- Green pepper, chopped – 1
- Hot pepper sauce – 1 tablespoon
- Fish sauce – 3 tablespoons
- Water – 1 tablespoon
- Sugar – ½ teaspoon
- Thai basil leaves (or just basil leaves) – 30 grams (check in oriental stores if your local supermarket does not provide).

Directions

1. Put the squid in a bowl and season with corn flour, salt, and pepper. After seasoning, set it aside for 15 minutes. After fifteen minutes are over, take a wok or a large frying pan and heat two tablespoons of oil over high heat.
2. In the hot oil, put the squid and stir-fry for 3-5 minutes until it becomes opaque. At this point, scoop it out and set it aside. Back to the wok/frying pan, heat another tablespoon of oil over high heat.
3. When hot, sprinkle the spring onions, garlic and shallot. Stir as you let them cook for 2-3 minutes until fragrance. Follow by adding onions together with salt and lower the heat to medium. Let it cook for 3-4 minutes so that the onions can soften.
4. When the onions soften, as you stir, put the fish sauce, hot pepper sauce, green pepper, sugar, and water.

5. Allow everything to cook for 1-2 minutes until they are all heated through. Are they ready? If they are, remove the wok from heat and serve.

41. Cucumber And Vietnamese Seafood

It is an impressive meal for the midweek. The cucumber blends well with shrimp sauce among other **ingredients** on the list.

Cooking time: 45 minutes
Serving: 4

Ingredients

- Small squid, scored (cut as if marking the flesh), cut into small pieces – 300 grams (¾ pounds)
- Tiger prawns, deveined – 300 grams (¾ pounds)
- Cucumber, slice into half, remove the seeds and cut into thin rods – 2
- Halved scallops – 4

- Large spring onions, cut white parts into rings and green parts broad diagonal slices, separate them – 2
- Finely chopped garlic cloves - 2
- Red chili, seed all, chop one to fine pieces and the other to broad pieces – 2
- Brown sugar – 2 teaspoons
- Shrimp sauce/paste – 1 tablespoons
- Halved limes – 3
- Frying oil
- Fish sauce – 1 tablespoon
- Coriander and mint, all chopped – 1 each or as preferred

Directions

1. Heat the wok over high heat. When heated, add a substantial amount of oil followed by the shrimp paste. Quickly fry for about a minute and then add the finely chopped chili, white parts of spring onions and garlic.
2. Once they are all in, cook as you stir the garlic and onions for one minute and then proceed to add the following: cucumber, fish sauce, sugar and a squeeze of one of the limes.
3. Add the seafood parts (squid and tiger prawns) and cook over the high heat for 2 minutes until they are all heated through. Is the seafood cooked through? Proceed to season with the sliced chili, half lime and green parts of the spring onions.

4. After a gentle stir, sprinkle the chopped coriander and mint and remove the wok from heat. You can also leave the cut parts (coriander and mint) on the side for the guests to season on their plates.

42. Seafood With Fried Rice

Cooking time: 25 minutes
Serving: 4

Ingredients

- White rice, cooked and ready to serve – 4 cups
- Lightly whisked egg – 1
- Onion, peel and cut into dices – 1
- Seafood marinara mix (from the store) – 500 grams
- Sliced garlic cloves – 2
- Carrot, diced into fine pieces – 1
- Broccoli, dice to small pieces – ½
- Frozen peas – 1 cup
- White mushrooms, button type, sliced – 100 grams (¼ pound)
- Soy sauce – 2 tablespoons
- Spring onions, sliced diagonally – 1
- Oyster sauce – 1 teaspoon

- Frying oil – 2 tablespoons
- Ground black pepper – 1

Directions

1. Take a small frying pan and heat a tablespoon of oil using medium heat. When the oil gets hot, add the egg as you stir in a circular motion. Continue stirring in the same motion until it appears set. You should reach a firm state before heading to the next step.
2. Once the egg is ready, remove it from the pan and let it cool off on a plate. After the heat release, roll the egg to form a cigar shape and slice it to create ribbons.
3. Now, it's time to switch to a bigger pan or a wok. Put oil in it (whatever you choose) and heat strongly. When the oil begins to simmer, immediately add the marinara mix. Start cooking as you stir for 3-4 minutes.
4. After the fourth minute, remove the mix from the wok/pan and put it aside. With the wok/pan in the same condition, put the onion and cook in a stirring manner for one minute before adding carrot and garlic.
5. Watch the garlic as it begins to color then add rice. Start tossing to mix and break any rice lumps formed in the process.
6. Once you are done tossing, add broccoli, peas, and mushrooms and go on to stir fry for the next 3-4 minutes.

7. When the mushrooms release their water, put the marinara mix back in the wok/frying pan. Add oyster and soy sauces then gently stir in the egg. Finally, season the seafood with pepper and spring onions before serving.

43. Garlic Seafood Marinara

Cooking time: 40 minutes
Serving: 4

Ingredients

- Seafood marinara mix – 600 grams
- Crushed garlic cloves – 4
- Ginger, peeled, cut into matchsticks – 1
- Carrot, peeled, into matchsticks – 1
- Celery salt (from the stores) – 1 teaspoon
- Peanut oil – 3 tablespoon

Sauce ingredients

- Chicken broth – ½ cup
- Oyster sauce – 2 tablespoons
- Water – ½ cup
- Sugar – 1 tablespoon
- Corn flour – 1 tablespoon
- Soy sauce – 1 tablespoon

Directions

1. Start by thoroughly mixing the sauce ingredients and put them aside. Once the mixture is ready, heat oil in a wok until it shimmers.
2. Proceed to add half of the crushed garlic clove and let it cook as you stir for 30 seconds.
3. After the garlic, add the seafood marinara mix. Stir-fry for 2-3 so that it is almost cooked. Is it ready? Remove the seafood mix from the wok and set it aside.
4. Without tampering with the wok, add more oil and heat vigorously.
5. When hot, put ginger and the remaining garlic in the wok. Stir-fry them for 30 seconds to one minute.
6. After the stir, add all the vegetables (leave out spring onions). Cook and stir for about two minutes until they are slightly soft. When the veggies soften, add the marinara back to the wok followed by spring onions.
7. Now, it's time to add the sauce prepared in step 1. Stir it briefly and add to the wok. Keep cooking as you stir until the seafood is cooked through making sure you have a thick sauce. Once everything is ready, turn off the heat and serve with steamed rice.

44. Chinese Fish Fillets

Cooking time: 25 minutes
Serving: 4

Ingredients

Fish ingredients

- Fish fillets, boneless, cut to bite size – 1 pound

Marinade ingredients

- Sesame oil – a few drops
- Sherry or white wine – 1 tablespoon
- Salt and pepper – as preferred
- Cornstarch – 2 teaspoons
- Egg white – 1 from a giant egg

Sauce ingredients

- Oyster sauce – 1 tablespoon

- Fish stock/chicken broth – ½ cup
- Cornstarch mixed with water – 1 teaspoon each
- Soy sauce – ¼ teaspoon
- Vegetable oil – 4 tablespoons
- Garlic cloves, minced – 1
- Red onion, sliced – ½
- Ginger, shredded – 2 slices
- Vegetables as desired (optional)
- Coriander, ground to taste – 2 teaspoons

Directions

Preparing the fish

1. Take a medium bowl and mix the following: sesame oil, wine, cornstarch, salt, and pepper.
2. After mixing, add fish to the mixture (marinade). Make sure it is well coated and let it sit for 10 minutes at room temperature.

Preparing the sauce

1. Take a small bowl and mix oyster and soy sauces with fish stock/chicken broth. After thorough mixing, put it aside.
2. Next, get a wok and heat two tablespoons of oil over high heat. When hot, remove the fish from the marinade, shaking off the excess and put in the wok.

3. After putting it in the wok, cook by stirring until the fish goes light brown. At this point, remove it from the wok and put it in a bowl. With the wok in the same condition, add ginger, garlic, and red onion. Cook until the onion is light brown.
4. When the onions are ready, add the vegetables (if included) and stir-fry. After the brief stir, pour in the sauce and heat until it bubbles.
5. After the sauce looks as if it is boiling, put the cornstarch and water mixture. Stir quickly so that it thickens. After thickening, return the fish to the wok and stir everything to mix. Finally, sprinkle the ground coriander, turn off the heat and serve.

Vegetables Stir-Fry Recipes

Plant-based recipes offer more nutritional value and everyone from your doctor to the next door neighbor recommends veggies for better health. So, it is the last chapter but not the least for the vegans.

Here are stir-fry recipes that will put a break on the meat.

45. Pak Choy/Bok Choy

Cooking time: 10 minutes
Serving: 4

Ingredients

- Pak/bok choy, rinsed, cut the head in half lengthwise – 4 medium heads
- Ginger knob, peeled and finely sliced – 2 teaspoons

- Vegetable oil – 2 tablespoons
- Garlic cloves, peeled, and finely sliced – 2 teaspoons
- Sugar – ½ teaspoon
- Scallions, finely chopped, white parts only – 1 ½ teaspoons
- Sesame oil – 1 teaspoon
- Kosher salt

Directions

1. Start by heating the oil in a wok using medium heat until it simmers.
2. Follow by adding the following: garlic, ginger, and scallions. After the addition, cook as you stir for a minute until they are aromatic.
3. When the smell reaches you, switch the heat to high. Proceed to add the choy and stir-fry for another minute until the outer leaves wilt.
4. After wilting, add sugar, then season with salt to taste. Once the salt is in, cook and stir for one more minute.
5. At this point, it is now ready. Remove the wok from heat and add the sesame oil. Season with more salt if it's okay with you before serving.

46. Lo Mein With Charred Cabbage, Shiitake, And Chives

Cooking time: 30 minutes
Serving: 4

Ingredients

- Lo Mein noodles (Chinese wheat flour noodles) – 1 pound
- Kosher salt
- Vegetable or canola oil – ¼ cup, divide equally
- Shiitake mushroom caps (resemble an umbrella), thinly sliced – 4 ounces (¼ pound)
- White cabbage, shredded – 4 cups
- Fresh garlic, minced – 1 tablespoon
- Chinese chives (or scallions), cut into 2-inch segments – 4 ounces (¼ pound)
- Ground white pepper – as preferred

- Light and dark soy sauces – 2 teaspoons each
- Roasted sesame oil – 1 tablespoon
- Shaoxing wine – 1 tablespoon

Directions

1. First, boil some salted water in a pot and then add the noodles. With the noodles in the pot, stir regularly with chopsticks or tongs for a minute, until they attain a firm state but separated.
2. When ready, drain the noodles and transfer them to a large bowl. Add a tablespoon of veggie oil to the noodle's bowl and toss before setting aside.
3. Now, it's time for the wok. Take it and heat a tablespoon of oil over high heat until it smokes. Add cabbage and then cook and stir regularly for 2 minutes until they are lightly brown in color.
4. At this point, the cabbages are ready to transfer to a bowl and setting aside. You don't have to clean the wok but do so if some of the cabbage chippings are still sticking around. Now, in the empty wok, put one tablespoon of oil and heat to smoke.
5. In the hot oil, add mushrooms and proceed to cook and stir for 2 minutes or so until they brown and are somehow crisp but tender. Join the mushrooms with the chives/scallions in a stirring manner for a minute until they lightly wilt. At wilting point, transfer them to the bowl containing cabbage.

6. Clean out the wok and then heat it before adding one more tablespoon of oil and wait until it smokes. Add the noodles and toss until they become hot.
7. Once the noodles are heated, add the cabbage, chives, mushrooms, and garlic. Toss them together with noodles for 30 seconds or until you smell the garlic.

8. After the 30-second toss, put the soy sauces, sesame oil, and wine. Cook as you toss and stir until the sauce coats the noodles. Finally, season with salt and white pepper before turning off the heat. Serve while it's still hot.

47. Smacked Cucumber

Cooking time: 50 minutes
Serving: 6

NB: You can serve it as a snack with drinks

Ingredients

- Frying oil
- Cucumber, cut into 4cm length, then chunk into wedges – 1
- Szechuan pepper – ½ teaspoon
- Red chili, dried and broken into pieces – 2
- Sesame oil

Directions

1. Take the cucumber pieces, one by one and smack them down using a cleaver's flat. Use your hands to do it. After crashing, remove the seeds and put the pieces in a sieve. Sprinkle a little salt to taste.

2. Let them settle for 30 minutes before rinsing and patting dry with paper towels. When the cucumbers are ready, heat some oil in a wok to smoking hot. In the hot oil, add chili and pepper. Follow by putting the smacked cucumber and stir for a minute.
3. After the minute, scoop the contents and put them on a plate. Remember to switch off the heat and remove the wok. Finally, sprinkle with sesame oil and serve.

48. Hoisin-Glazed Tofu (Bean Curd) And Brown Rice

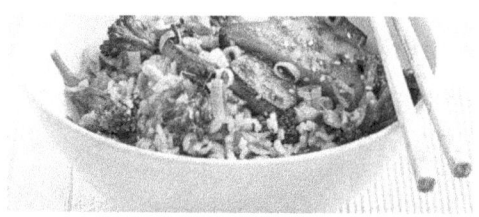

Cooking time: 30 minutes plus an hour of pressing
Serving: 2

Ingredients

- Hoisin sauce – 4 tablespoons
- Firm tofu (bean curd) – 400 grams (1 pound)
- Sesame seeds – 2 teaspoons
- Crushed garlic cloves – 2
- Grated ginger – 2 teaspoons
- Sesame oil
- Red chili, seeded, cut into dices – 1
- Spring onions, finely sliced – 1 bunch
- Brown rice, cooked – 250 grams
- Soya beans – 50 grams
- Broccoli, briefly cooked and chopped – 200 grams (½ pound)
- Soy sauce – 1 tablespoon

Directions

1. Start by cutting the tofu into strips (wide ones are preferred) and put them between two kitchen towel sheets.
2. Now you have a sandwiched tofu. Press the cut strips down using a chopping board to release some water. After the hard press, it's now ready for the next step.
3. In this step, you need the grill. Put a baking sheet with oil on it and heat it strongly before pouring the pressed tofu by brushing together with half of the hoisin.
4. Once they are all on the baking sheet, season on top with a teaspoon of sesame seeds and then grill the contents for 6-8 minutes until they turn crisp and golden.
5. Now, turn the tofu coat and add more hoisin. It's okay if you feel like scattering some more sesame seeds. Cook over the grill until you get a fragile nature before setting the tofu aside in a bowl.
6. In another setting, fry the garlic, ginger, and chili using a teaspoon of sesame oil in a wok until aromatic.
7. Next, add spring onions to the wok and stir-fry for one minute. After the onions soften, add rice and fry it for five minutes to heat through.
8. After the fifth minute, add soya and broccoli followed by soy sauce seasoning. Put the contents

in bowls and top with tofu. Scatter the remaining spring onions on top and serve.

49. Aubergine (Eggplant) And Sesame Seeds

Cooking time: 30 minutes
Serving: 2

Ingredients

- Aubergines/eggplant, cut into wedges – 2 small ones
- Sliced spring onions – 2
- Sesame oil
- Crushed garlic cloves – 3
- Ginger, shredded – thumb size
- Soy sauce – 1 tablespoon
- Mirin – 1 tablespoon
- Rice wine vinegar or dry sherry – 1 tablespoon
- Sesame seeds – 1 teaspoon
- Corn flour – 1 teaspoon

Directions

1. Take a wok and heat a tablespoon of oil. When hot, stir in ginger, garlic, chili and almost all spring onions for two minutes or until aromatic.
2. Once you reach the fragrance stage, add the eggplant together with water splash. Let them simmer for 10-15 minutes to soften.
3. Add more heat and follow by putting soy sauce, vinegar, and mirin. After the addition, cook until half of the liquid is evaporated.
4. As evaporation progresses, take a bowl and mix corn flour with water splash. When you get an even mixture, stir it in the wok for two more minutes.
5. After the stir, scatter the remaining spring onions, sesame seeds, and chili slices. At this point, it is ready to serve with rice.

50. Stir-Fry Vegetables

Cooking time: 20 minutes
Serving: 4

Ingredients

- Broccoli florets – 3 cups
- PLANTERS peanut oil (check the store) – 2 tablespoons
- Red pepper, cut into strips – 1 cup
- Water chestnuts (also known as Chinese water chestnuts), drained and sliced – 1 can
- Green onions, cut into slices – 3
- A.1. original sauce (produced by Kraft Foods since 1831) – 3 tablespoons
- Lemon juice – 1 teaspoon
- Soy sauce – 1 tablespoon
- Frying oil

Directions

1. Take a wok and heat a substantial amount of oil over medium to high heat.
2. Wait for the oil to get hot before putting broccoli, onions, and pepper. Once they are all in, cook and stir for 8 minutes until the ingredients are crisp but tender.
3. After the eighth minute, put as you stir all the remaining ingredients and cook for 3-5 minutes. At this point, they are heated through. Don't stop stirring during this period. Are they ready? Turn off the heat and serve.

51. Sesame Vegetables With Rice

Cooking time: 35 minutes
Serving: 3

Ingredients

- Long-grain rice, uncooked – ¾ cup
- Vegetable broth – 1 ½ cups
- Fresh asparagus, trim and cut into 1-inch pieces – ½ pound
- Sesame seeds – 1 tablespoon
- Margarine – 1 tablespoon
- Peanut oil – 2 tablespoons (preferred but you can use vegetable oil, same amount)
- Large red bell pepper, cut into 1-inch pieces – 1
- Mushrooms, sliced – 2 cups
- Yellow onion, sliced – 1, large one
- Fresh and minced ginger root – 2 teaspoons
- Soy sauce – 3 tablespoons
- Minced garlic – 1 teaspoon
- Sesame oil – 1 tablespoon

Directions

1. First, you need the oven. Heat it to 175 degrees Celsius (350 degrees F). Next, take a saucepan and combine rice with broth and margarine. Cover them and heat in the oven until they boil.
2. At boiling point, reduce the heat so that the rice simmers for 15 minutes. Set the rice aside when all the liquid is absorbed.
3. Now, it's time to prepare the sesame seeds. Put them on a baking sheet and heat in the preheated oven for 5-6 minutes so that they turn golden brown. After attaining a golden color, put them aside in a separate bowl or plate.
4. With the seeds ready, head for the wok or skillet. Take it and heat the peanut oil using the medium to high heat.
5. In the hot oil, add asparagus, onion, bell pepper, ginger, mushrooms, and garlic. Proceed to stir-fry them for 4-5 minutes until the veggies become tender but still crisp. The above inputs are followed by stirring in the soy sauce and let it cook for 30 seconds.
6. After the sauce, turn off the heat. While it's still hot, put toasted sesame seeds and sesame oil and stir before serving over the rice.

52. Garbanzo

Cooking time: 35 minutes
Serving: 3

Ingredients

- Rinsed and drained Garbanzo beans – 1 can
- Fresh oregano (of the mint family), chopped – 1 tablespoon
- Olive oil – 2 tablespoons
- Fresh and chopped basil – 1 tablespoon
- Black pepper, ground – as preferred
- Crushed garlic cloves – 1
- Large zucchini, half and slice it – 1
- Fresh coriander or cilantro (same family), chopped – 1 tablespoon
- Sliced mushrooms – ½ cup
- Chopped tomato – 1

Directions

1. Take a large skillet/wok and heat oil using medium heat. In the hot oil, put oregano, garlic, basil, and pepper and keep stirring as you put each of the ingredients.
2. After stirring all the ingredients, add zucchini and garbanzo beans and stir everything to coat.
3. Next, cover the food and let it cook but keep stirring once in a while. It should take you 10 minutes.
4. When ten minutes are over, put the cilantro/coriander and mushrooms in a stirring motion. Continue to stir as the mixture cooks until they reach a tender state. When the mushrooms tenderize, place the tomato on the mixture and don't mix.
5. Cover the food and let the tomato steam for some minutes. Don't allow it to get mushy. When the food is ready, turn off the heat and serve while it's still hot.

53. Broccoli Noodles And Spicy Mushroom

Cooking time: 20 minutes
Serving: 2

Ingredients

- Vegetable stock cube, with low-salt – 1
- Small head broccoli florets – 1
- Medium egg noodles – 2 nests (about 125 grams)
- Shiitake/chestnut mushroom, cut into thick slices – 250 grams
- Sesame oil – 1 tablespoon, preserve more for serving
- Large garlic clove, chopped – 1
- Thinly sliced spring onions – 4
- Dried chili, break down into pieces – ½ teaspoon
- Hoisin sauce – 2 tablespoons
- Roasted cashew nuts – a handful

Directions

1. Start by putting water in a pan and boil the vegetable stock cube. At boiling point, add egg noodles and then let them simmer together for 2 minutes.
2. After the second minute, put broccoli in the pan and let it boil for another two minutes. When ready, turn off the heat and reserve a cup of the 'stock broth' before draining the rest.
3. Next, heat a wok/large non-stick frying pan and add sesame oil and mushrooms. Stir-fry them for two minutes until they turn golden.
4. After the mushrooms stir, add chili flakes, garlic, and almost all spring onions. Cook them for a minute before adding the boiled broccoli and noodles.
5. Once the noodles and broccoli are in, splash three tablespoons of the reserved stock. Follow by putting hoisin sauce and toss for another minute using two wooden spoons or a pair of tongs.
6. When everything is ready, turn off the heat and serve the noodles sprinkled with the toasted cashew nuts and the rest of spring onions. If it's okay, you can add some sesame oil for the taste.

54. Seitan (Wheat Gluten) And Black Bean

Cooking time: 45 minutes
Serving: 4

Ingredients

Sauce ingredients

- Dark brown sugar, soft granules – 75 grams (about 0.2 pounds)
- Rinsed and drained black beans – 400 grams
- Garlic cloves – 3
- Chinese five-spice (check the stores) – 1 teaspoon
- Soy sauce – 2 tablespoons
- Rice vinegar – 2 tablespoons
- Red chili, chop into fine pieces – 1
- Smooth peanut butter – 1 tablespoon

Stir-fry ingredients

- Corn flour – 1 tablespoon
- Marinated seitan (wheat gluten) pieces – 350 grams
- Sliced red pepper – 1
- Vegetable oil – 3 tablespoons
- Chopped pak choi – 300 grams (¾ pounds)
- Sliced spring onions – 2
- Rice or rice noodles, cooked and ready to serve.

Directions

1. In the food processor bowl, prepare the sauce by putting beans and ingredients in the sauce section. Add 50ml of water and blend to a smooth texture.
2. When blended, pour the sauce into a saucepan and gently heat for five minutes until thick and shiny before setting it aside in a bowl.
3. Next, drain the seitan and dry with paper towels. Put the pieces in a bowl with corn flour and toss before setting the coated seitan pieces aside.
4. After the coating exercise, heat a wok over high heat then add some oil and seitan in batches.
5. Cook and stir them for 5 minutes until the edges turn golden brown. After the color turn, use a slotted spoon to remove the seitan from the wok and put aside in a plate.
6. Now, dry the empty wok and add a teaspoon of vegetable oil. Wait for the oil to heat before putting all the beans, pepper, spring onions and pak choi.

Once they are all in, cook them in a stirring manner for 3-4 minutes.
7. After the fourth minute, return the seitan and stir to coat with the sauce before letting it boil for a minute. Finally, when everything is ready, switch off the heat and serve together with rice or noodles.

55. Gingered Tofu, Pea Noodles And Aubergine (Eggplant)

Cooking time: 25 minutes
Serving: 4

Ingredients

- Aubergines/eggplant, cut into small chunks – 2
- Toasted sesame oil – 3 tablespoons
- Garlic cloves – 1
- Medium egg noodles – 4 nests (about 250 grams)
- Grated ginger – thumb size
- Soy sauce – 3 tablespoons
- Chinese five-spice powder – 2 teaspoons (from the stores or check on how to make one)
- Marinated tofu (bean curd) pieces – 160 grams (0.4 pounds)
- Sweet chili sauce – 3 tablespoons
- Spring onions, shred – 3

- Frozen peas (unfrozen) – 225 grams (about ½ pound)

Directions

1. First, cook the noodles according to package instructions. When the noodles are ready, take a wok, or a large non-stick frying pan and heat over high heat then add two tablespoons of oil.
2. In the hot oil, put the aubergine/eggplant pieces and proceed to cook and stir them for 8-10 minutes until they turn brown and completely soft. At this point, remove the eggplant pieces from the wok/frying pan and add the remaining tablespoon of oil.
3. Wait for the oil to get hot before putting ginger and garlic. Let them cook for 30 seconds without stirring. Then, as you stir, put the five-spice.
4. Next, with the help of a spoon, put the chili and soy sauces then stir as you let it bubble for another 30 seconds. After the bubble, toss in the tofu, eggplant pieces, and peas. Cook as you stir until they are all heated through.
5. Before you serve, add the noodles and toss to mix everything. Finally, turn off the heat and serve in the respective bowls. Let the guests season with spring onions on their plates as desired.

Part 2

Introduction

Stir-fries are one of the most popular and delicious Chinese dishes around. Except from being very easy and fast to prepare, stir - fry dishes are based on lean meats, vegetables, fruits and roots which makes them a highly nutritious meal full of good quality protein, essential fatty acids, vitamins, minerals, trace minerals, fibre and powerful antioxidants. This book contains a total of 30 healthy and colourful stir fry recipes for lunch and dinner that will keep you healthy while providing you with the unique flavour and aroma of traditional Asian cuisine.

Velvet Chicken & Cashew Nut Stir Fry

Ingredients

1 large egg white
1 tbsp cornstarch
4 tbsp vegetable oil
500 grams chicken breast, excess fat removed
1 cup broccoli florets
2 tbsp whole cashew nuts
2 tbsp. light soy sauce
1 tsp grated ginger
1 garlic clove, minced
1.5 cups rice, cooked to package instructions

Preparation

1. Thinly slice the chicken breasts.
2. In a large bowl, combine the egg white and corn starch; mix well to dissolve.
3. Coat the chicken with the egg – corn starch mixture and place in a sealed container. Refrigerate for 30 minutes.
4. In a wok or large skillet, heat vegetable oil over high

heat

5. Add the chicken and stir-fry for 2-3 minutes or until golden.
6. Add broccoli and stir-fry for 2 minutes or until tender crisp. Toss and stir constantly.
7. In small bowl, combine the soy sauce, garlic and ginger.
8. Add to wok together with the cashew nuts and stir-fry for about 1 minute.
9. Serve and enjoy.

Spicy Salmon Stir Fry

Ingredients

3 tbsp peanut oil
400 grams organic salmon fillets
1 cup broccoli florets
1 cup green beans
1 tbsp. oyster sauce
1 red bell pepper, cored, seeded, and thinly sliced
1 tsp clear honey
¼ tsp chilli flakes
1 garlic clove, minced
1.5 cups rice, cooked to package instructions
Salt and pepper to taste

Preparation

1. Cut the salmon fillets into cubes.
2. In a wok or large skillet, heat peanut oil over high heat
3. Add the salmon and stir-fry for 2-3 minutes until both sides are golden.

4. Remove from wok and set aside.
5. Thinly slice the bell pepper
6. In a large bowl combine the bell pepper slices, broccoli florets and green beans together with the oyster sauce, honey, chillies and garlic.
7. Add to wok and stir-fry for 2-3 minutes or until tender crisp. Toss and stir constantly.
8. Add the salmon cubes.
9. Season with salt and pepper.

Stir Fried Teriyaki Tofu

Ingredients

200 grams extra firm tofu
1 cup snow peas
3 tbsp sesame oil
1 tbsp rice wine
1 tbsp honey
3 tbsp. low sodium soy sauce
1 tsp grated ginger
1.5 cups rice, cooked to package instructions

Preparation

1. Cut tofu into cubes and pat dry.
2. In a large bowl combine rice wine, honey, soy sauce and grated ginger.
3. Marinade tofu in the mixture for at least one hour, preferably overnight.
4. Heat the sesame oil in a large wok or frying pan over medium heat.
5. Add the tofu and stir-fry for 2 minutes.

6. Add the peas and stir-fry for 2 more minutes.
7. Serve.

Ginger & Lime Infused King Prawn Stir Fry

Ingredients

3 tbsp coconut oil
250 grams tiger prawns, cooked and peeled
2 cups Brussel sprouts
2 spring onions, finely chopped
2 tbsp. soy sauce
½ tsp grated ginger
2 tbsp lime juice
1 tbsp chopped fresh coriander leaves
½ garlic clove, minced
Salt and pepper to taste

Preparation

1. In a wok or large skillet, heat coconut oil over high heat.
2. Add the prawns and stir-fry for 2-3 minutes until both sides are golden.
3. Add the rest of the ingredients and stir-fry for 2-3

minutes or until tender crisp. Toss and stir constantly.
4. Serve and enjoy.

Healthy Quinoa Stir Fry

Ingredients

1 tsp vegetable oil
1 cup broccoli florets
1 cup red cabbage, shredded
1 cup green beans
½ cup quinoa
1.5 cup water
2 tbsp pine nuts
2 tbsp fresh mint, chopped
2 tbsp fresh coriander, chopped
2 tbsp soy sauce

Preparation

1. In a pot, bring water to a boil and add the quinoa. Cook until all the water is absorbed or until quinoa is cooked.
2. Toast the pine nuts in a dry frying pan until golden.
3. In a wok or large skillet, heat vegetable oil over high heat.

4. Add the vegetables and stir-fry for 2-3 minutes until tender crisp.
5. In a small bowl, combine the soy sauce, coriander and mint and pour over the vegetables. Stir constantly for 1 minute.
6. Serve and enjoy.

Smoked Salmon & Bean Sprout Stir Fry

Ingredients

3 tbsp peanut oil
50 grams smoked salmon
2 cups bean sprouts
2 cups broccoli florets

2 tbsp soy sauce
1 red chilli, chopped
1/2 sweet onion, sliced thin
½ tsp grated ginger
1 garlic clove, minced

Preparation

1. In a wok or large skillet, heat peanut oil over high heat.
2. Combine all the ingredients together and add to wok.

3. Stir-fry for 2-3 minutes. Toss and stir constantly.
4. Serve and enjoy.

Mushroom & Ostrich Stir Fry

Ingredients

3 tbsp vegetable oil
400 grams ostrich steak
2 cups broccoli florets
2 spring onions, finely chopped
2 tbsp. soy sauce
½ tsp grated ginger
½ garlic clove, minced
1 tsp tossed sesame seeds

Preparation

1. Cut the ostrich steaks into medium sized cubes.
2. In a wok or large skillet, heat vegetable oil over high heat.
3. Add the ostrich cubes and stir-fry for 3-4 minutes until both sides are golden.
4. Add the rest of the ingredients and stir-fry for 2-3 minutes or until broccoli is tender crisp.
5. Enjoy.

Exotic Mango And Mushroom Stir Fry

Ingredients

3 tbsp coconut oil
2 cups button mushrooms
1 cup mango cut into cubes
2 cups broccoli florets
2 tbsp soy sauce
2 spring onions, thinly chopped
½ tsp grated ginger
½ garlic clove, minced
1 fresh lemongrass stalk

Preparation

1. In a wok or large skillet, heat coconut oil over high heat.
2. Combine all the ingredients together and add to wok.
3. Stir-fry for 2-3 minutes. Toss and stir constantly.
4. Serve and enjoy.

Chicken And Fig Stir Fry

Ingredients

3 tbsp vegetable oil
400 grams chicken breast, cut into thin slices
1 cup green beans
½ cup fresh figs, halved
2 spring onions, thinly chopped
2 tbsp fresh coriander, chopped
1 red chilli, thinly chopped
1 tbsp soy sauce
1 tbsp Worcester sauce
½ tsp grated ginger
1 kafir lime leaf
Pepper to taste

Preparation

1. In a wok or large skillet, heat vegetable oil over high heat.
2. Combine all the ingredients together except figs.

3. Add to wok and stir-fry for 3 minutes or until green beans are tender crisp.
4. Toss and stir constantly.
5. Add figs.
6. Stir for 1 minute.
7. Serve

Thai Red Curry Stir Fry

Ingredients

3 tbsp coconut oil
200 grams shrimps, cooked and peeled
2 cups snow peas
1 medium sized onion, thinly sliced
1 red chilli, thinly chopped
2 tsp red curry powder
2 tbsp low sodium soy sauce
½ tsp grated ginger
2 tsp tomato paste
1 kafir lime leaf
Pepper to taste

Preparation

1. In a wok or large skillet, heat coconut oil over medium heat.

2. Once the oil is hot, add the spring onion, curry powder and ginger. Cook for 1 minute.

3. Add the shrimps and stir-fry for 2-3 minutes or until thoroughly cooked.

4. Combine all the rest ingredients together.
5. Add to wok and stir-fry for 1 more minute or until snow peas are tender crisp.
6. Toss and stir constantly.
7. Enjoy.

Chicken Stir Fry With Hoi Sin Sauce

Ingredients

3 tbsp sesame oil
400 grams chicken breast, cut into thin slices
2 cups spring onions, chopped
2 cups cucumber sticks
3 tbsp hoi sin sauce
½ tsp grated ginger
½ tsp sesame seeds
Pepper to taste

Preparation

1. In a wok or large skillet, heat oil over high heat.
2. Add chicken and cook thoroughly for 3-4 minutes.
3. Add the rest of the ingredients except sesame seeds.
4. Stir- fry until cucumbers are tender-crisp to the bite (about 3 minutes).
5. Place on a serving plate and top with sesame seeds.

Delicious Coconut Pork

Ingredients

3 tbsp coconut oil
400 grams lean pork, cut into cube
½ cup mango cubes
1 cup whole button mushrooms
1 red bell pepper, thinly sliced
2 tbsp soy sauce
4 tbsp coconut milk
½ tsp grated ginger
Salt and pepper to taste
Preparation

1. In a wok or large skillet, heat coconut oil over high heat.
2. Add pork and cook thoroughly for 3-4 minutes.
3. Add the rest of the ingredients except coconut milk
4. Stir- fry until call vegetables are tender-crisp to the bite (aproximately 3 minutes).

5. When ready, add coconut milk.
6. Stir well for 1 minute.
7. Remove from heat.
8. Serve.

Prawn And Pineapple On Coconut Rice

Ingredients

3 tbsp coconut oil
400 grams tiger prawns, cooked and peeled
1 cup pineapple chunks
1 cup coconut milk
1 cup jasmine rice
2 tbsp fresh coriander, chopped
2 tbsp oyster sauce
Pepper to taste

Preparation

1. Add rice, coconut milk and 2 cups water in a medium saucepan. Bring to a boil, cover and reduce heat to low.
2. Cook until rice is tender and liquid is absorbed (approximately 40 minutes).
3. In a wok or large skillet, heat oil over high heat.
4. Add prawns and stir fry for 1 minute.
5. Add the rest of the ingredients.
6. Toss and stir constantly for 1 more minute.

7. Place on a serving plate on top of coconut rice and serve hot.

Healthy Beef Stir Fry

Ingredients

1 tbsp olive oil
400 grams lean beef, cut into strips
½ cup broccoli
1 cup red pepper
1 cup green beans
½ onion, chopped
½ tsp sesame seeds
1-2 tbsp light soy sauce
½ tsp fresh ginger, grated
Salt and pepper to taste

Preparation

1. In a wok or non-stick frying pan warm the olive oil, add the beef and sauté for about 2 minutes.
2. Add the rest of the ingredients except sesame seeds.
3. Stir- fry vegetables are tender-crisp to the bite (about 3 minutes).

4. Place on a serving plate and top with sesame seeds.
5. Enjoy.

Vegetarian Apple-Cinnamon And Brussel Sprout Stir Fry

Ingredients

2 tsp coconut oil
2 cups Brussel sprouts
1 medium sized apple, cut into small cubes
2 cups spring onions, chopped
2 tbsp light soy sauce
1 tsp clear honey
1/3 tsp grated cinnamon
½ tsp grated ginger

Preparation

1. In a wok or large skillet, heat coconut oil over high heat.
2. In a small bowl combine honey, soy sauce, cinnamon and ginger.
3. Add the rest of the ingredients in the wok.

4. Stir- fry for 2 minutes.
5. Pour the honey, soy sauce, cinnamon and ginger.
6. Stir fry for 1 more minute.
7. Serve and enjoy.

Superfood Stir Fry

Ingredients

2 tbsp olive oil
2 large salmon fillets cut into cubes
2 cups broccoli florets
½ tsp chilli flakes
½ tsp lime juice
2 tbsp soy sauce
½ tsp fresh ginger, grated
1.5 cups noodles, cooked to package instructions

Preparation

1. In a wok or non-stick frying pan warm the olive oil, add the salmon and sauté for about 2 minutes.
2. Add the lime juice and stir for 1 more minute.
3. Add the rest of the ingredients.
4. Stir- fry for 2-3 minutes or until broccoli florets are tender-crisp.
5. Serve.
6. Enjoy.

Delicious Mussel Stir Fry

Ingredients

3 tbsp sesame oil
500 grams mussels, cooked
2 cups spring onions, chopped
1 cup cabbage, shredded
4 tbsp chopped coriander
2 tsp tomato paste
½ tsp grated ginger
Salt and pepper to taste

Preparation

1. In a wok or large skillet, heat oil over high heat.
2. Add mussels and stir fry for 2 minutes.
3. Add the rest of the ingredients except coriander.
4. Stir-fry for 2 more minutes.
5. Place on a serving plate and garnish with coriander.
6. Serve and enjoy.

Nutty Stir Fry

Ingredients

200 grams lean beef cut into thin strips
3 tbsp peanut oil
½ cup Brazil nuts
2 cups broccoli florets
2 cups cucumber sticks
2 tbsp light soy sauce
1 tbsp rice wine
½ tsp garlic powder
½ tsp grated ginger
Pepper to taste

Preparation

1. In a wok or large skillet, heat oil over high heat.
2. Add beef and for 1-2 minutes.
3. Add the rest of the ingredients except.
4. Stir- fry until broccoli florets are tender-crisp to the bite (about 3 minutes).
5. Serve and enjoy.

Mediterranean Style Stir Fry

Ingredients

400 grams shrimps, cooked and peeled
3 tbsp olive oil
½ cup cherry tomatoes, halved
1 medium sized courgette, thinly sliced
2 tbsp oyster sauce
1 tsp tomato puree
½ tsp garlic powder
½ tsp dried oregano
Pepper to taste

Preparation

1. In a wok or large skillet, heat olive oil over high heat.
2. Add the shrimps and stir-fry for 1 minute.
3. Add the tomatoes and courgette and stir-fry for 1 more minute.
4. Toss and stir constantly.
5. In small bowl, combine the oyster sauce, tomato

puree, garlic and oregano and add to wok together with the shrimps, cherry tomatoes and courgette slices.
6. Stir-fry for about 2 minutes.
7. Serve and enjoy.

Octopus Stir Fry

Ingredients

400 grams octopus
3 tbsp sesame oil
2 orange bell peppers, thinly sliced
2 spring onions, thinly chopped
2 tbsp soy sauce
1 tbsp rice wine
½ tsp garlic powder
½ tsp grated ginger
½ tsp turmeric
1 tsp tomato puree
Pepper to taste

Preparation

1. In a wok or large skillet, heat sesame oil over high heat.
2. Add octopus and stir-fry for 2-3 minutes or until thoroughly cooked.
3. Add the rest of the ingredients.
4. Stir- fry for 2-3 minutes or until pepper slices

become soft.
5. Serve and enjoy.

Vegan Stir Fry

Ingredients

3 cups cooked chickpeas
3 tbsp sunflower oil
2 medium sized tomatoes cut into small cubes
1 cup baby spinach
1 large onion, chopped
1 garlic clove, minced
2 tbsp rice vinegar
½ tsp garlic powder
¼ tsp cumin seeds
Salt and pepper to taste

Preparation

1. In a wok or large skillet, heat sunflower oil over medium heat.
2. Add onion and sauté for 1-2 minutes or until golden.
3. Add the rest of the ingredients except spinach.
4. Stir- fry for 1 minute stirring constantly.

5. Add spinach and stir fry for 1 more minute.
6. Enjoy.

Colorful Stir Fry With Bamboo Shoots

Ingredients

3 tbsp canola oil
200 grams chicken breast, cut into thin slices
1 green bell pepper, thinly sliced
1 red bell pepper, thinly sliced
½ cup baby carrots
½ cup baby corn
1 medium sized sweet onion, thinly sliced
½ cup broccoli florets
½ cup bamboo shoots
½ tsp grated ginger
1 tbsp light soy sauce
1 tbsp oyster sauce
1 tsp lime juice
Pepper to taste
Preparation

1. In a wok or large skillet, heat oil over high heat.
2. Add chicken and cook thoroughly for 3-4 minutes.
3. Add the rest of the ingredients and stir-fry for 3 more minutes or until vegetables are tender-crisp to the bite.
4. Serve and enjoy.

Coconut, Feta & Spinach Stir Fry

Ingredients

2 tbsp coconut oil
5 cups baby spinach
1.5 cup spring onions, chopped
2 cups feta cheese cut into small cubes
½ tsp grated ginger
1 garlic clove, minced
2 tbsp coconut cream
Salt and pepper to taste

Preparation

1. In a wok or large skillet, heat coconut oil over high heat.
2. In a large bowl combine all ingredients except coconut milk.
3. Place in wok and stir fry for 2 minutes.
4. Place on a serving plate and top with coconut cream. Mix well to combine.
5. Serve.

Spicy Beef Noodles

Ingredients

2 tbsp coconut oil
4 cups Chinese egg noodles
1 cup spring onions, chopped
200 grams lean beef cut into thin strips
½ tsp grated ginger
1 garlic clove, minced
½ tsp sesame seeds
2 tbsp light soy sauce
½ tsp sweet paprika
½ tsp chilli flakes
Salt and pepper

Preparation

1. Cook noodles in a large pan of boiling water 3 minutes or until done and drain in a colander over a bowl.

2. In a wok or large skillet, heat coconut oil over medium heat.
   Add beef strips and cook for 2-3 minutes.
   Remove from heat and set aside.
   Add the rest of the ingredients.
   Stir fry for 2 minutes.
   Add noodles and beef.
   Stir fry for 1 more minute.
   Serve and enjoy!

Stir Fry Recipes

1) Stir Fry With Ground Beef

Prep Time: 10 minutes
Cook Time: 10 minutes
Ready In: 20 minutes
Servings: 4

INGREDIENTS:

2 cups cooked rice, cold
1/2 lb. ground beef
1 Tbs. vegetable oil
2 eggs, well beaten
1 tsp. fresh ginger, minced
1 scallion, chopped
1 medium carrot, finely chopped
1 celery rib, finely chopped
1 clove garlic, minced
2 Tbs. soy sauce
1/2 tsp. sugar

DIRECTIONS:

1. Scramble the eggs. Set aside. Mix sugar, salt, pepper and soy sauce in a separate bowl. Set aside.

2. Sauté the ground beef with carrot, celery and scallion for

3. 3 minutes; stir occasionally until turn into brown. Put the garlic and ginger and cook for 1 minute. Add in the rice; fry for 1 minute. Whisk in the soy sauce mixture and the scrambled eggs then continue stirring for 30 seconds and serve.

2) Stir Fry With Chinese Sausage

Prep Time: 20 minutes
Cook Time: 15 minutes
Ready In: 35 minutes
Servings: 2-3

INGREDIENTS:

1 cup rice (raw)
1 cup of any type of chopped meat (shrimp, chicken, beef, Chinese sausage)
1/2 cup of frozen mix veggies
2 stalks green onion chopped
1/4 stick of unsalted butter chopped
2 cloves of garlic minced
1 teaspoon of white pepper
1-2 eggs beaten
1 teaspoon of salt
2 Tablespoons of soy sauce
2 Tablespoons of fish sauce

DIRECTIONS:

1.
Scramble the eggs, put in the frozen veggies and fry. Set aside.

2.

Cook the Chinese sausage, if ready, add the rice and stir constantly. Add the mixed egg and veggies, butter and onion. Stir evenly for few more minutes. Season it with salt to taste and serve

3) Stir Fry With Bean Sprout

Prep Time: 10 minutes
Cook Time: 15 minutes
Ready In: 25 minutes
Servings: 4

INGREDIENTS:

3 cups cooked, cooled doongara long-grain rice
1 1/2 cups beansprouts, trimmed
3 1/2 cups skinless shredded barbecued chicken
1/3 cup shredded fresh basil leaves
1 large red onion, cut into thin wedges
2 medium (300g) carrots, peeled, cut into matchsticks
100g snow peas, trimmed, thinly sliced lengthways
2 tablespoons soy sauce
olive oil cooking spray

DIRECTIONS:

1. Cook the onion, put in the chicken and carrots and leave it for 1-2 minutes until evenly heated.
2. Fold in the rice, beansprouts and snow peas and cook for 1-2 minutes. Stir in with soy sauce and garlic. When cooked, top it with basil and serve.

4)Stir Fry With Lemon And Butter

Prep Time: 15 minutes
Cook Time: 30 minutes
Ready In: 45 minutes
Servings: 4

INGREDIENTS:

Rice – 2 cups Water – 4 cups
Butter – 3 tablespoon
Lemon juice – 2 teaspoon
Cooked Chicken, prawns & egg – 1/2 cup each
Cooked Carrot & Peas – 1/2 cup
Soya sauce – 1 tablespoon
Salt
Oil

DIRECTIONS:

1.Add the rice to the melted rice, stir-fry evenly. Put in the boiled lemon juice, water and salt wait until the rice is well cooked. Set aside.
2.In a separate pan; fry prawns, eggs, cooked vegetables and chicken whisk with soya sauce and cook for 5 minutes. Put in the rice and mix well. Best if served hot.

5) Stir Fry With Oyster Sauce

Prep Time: 10 minutes
Cook Time: 10 minutes
Ready In: 20 minutes
Servings: 4-6

INGREDIENTS:

4 cups cold cooked rice
Seasonings (add according to taste)
1/2 cup green peas
1 medium onion, diced
1 green onion, diced
8 ounces cooked chicken (or substitute cooked turkey, etc.), chopped
2 eggs (more if desired)
Light Soy Sauce
Oyster sauce
Pepper
Salt
Oil for stir-frying, as needed

DIRECTIONS:

1.
Fry the beaten eggs upside down. Cut the egg into thin strips and set aside. Fry the onion and green peas separately and set aside.
2.

Stir the fried rice, season with salt, pepper and oyster sauce. Mix in chicken, onion and cooked green peas, stir thoroughly. Serve the fried rice and top it with egg strips and green onions.

6) Stir Fry With Duck

Prep Time: 10 minutes
Cook Time: 35 minutes
Ready In: 45 minutes
Servings: 6

INGREDIENTS:

2 cups long-grain rice
1 confit duck leg and thigh, skinned and boned
2 teaspoons garam masala or curry powder
1 medium-size onion, finely chopped
4 ounces smoked country bacon, diced
4 scallions, trimmed and minced
Freshly ground black pepper
2 large eggs, lightly beaten
2 tablespoons peanut oil
1 tablespoon soy sauce
Salt to taste

DIRECTIONS:

1.
Cook the rice and refrigerate it for 30 minutes. In a separate bowl, mix the shredded duck meat with soy sauce and pepper, set aside.
2.
Cook the bacon until it turned light brown. Set Aside. Fry onion and whisk in the garam masala or

curry powder. Add in the eggs and combine it evenly then put in the mixed duck meat, cooked bacon and rice. Cook in a medium heat and stir thoroughly.
3.
Serve the fried rice and scatter the scallions on top.

7) Stir Fry With Peanuts

Prep Time: 20 minutes
Cook Time: 10 minutes
Ready In: 30 minutes
Servings: 4

INGREDIENTS:

4 cups cooked long-grain white rice
1/2 cup chopped peanuts, for garnish
6 tablespoons peanut oil
1/2 small head napa cabbage, core removed and finely sliced
1/2 pound medium shrimp, peeled and deveined
1 (2-inch) piece ginger, peeled and grated
1/2 cup frozen peas, thawed in warm water
3 tablespoons soy sauce
1/4 bunch scallions, sliced, for garnish
2 cloves garlic, minced
3 large eggs, lightly beaten
2 shallots, thinly sliced
Salt

DIRECTIONS:

1.
Stir-fry the shallots and ginger with the peanut oil and wait until fragrant. Add in the cabbage and cook it for

about 8 minutes. Put in some salt to taste and set aside.

2.

Put 2 tablespoons of oil in the skillet and when heated add in the garlic and wait until fragrant. Add the shrimp and leave it cooked for 2-3 minutes and set aside.

3.

Scramble the eggs lightly, add the rice and mix thoroughly. Fold in the cooked cabbage and shrimp and the peas. Season to taste.

4.

Remove from heat and serve with peanuts and scallions scattered on top.

8) Stir Fry With Salmon

Prep Time: 5 minutes
Cook Time: 30 minutes
Ready In: 35 minutes
Servings: 2

INGREDIENTS:

2 bowls of Japanese rice (no more than 2 bowls per batch)
1 fresh salmon or leftover Salted Salmon (shiojake)
Freshly ground black pepper (to taste)
1/8 tsp. white pepper (to taste)
1/4 tsp. salt (to taste)
2 Tbsp. vegetable oil
1 Tbsp. sesame oil
1 tsp. soy sauce
1 green onion
1-2 egg(s)
Salt

DIRECTIONS:

1.
Break the baked salmon into bits and set aside. Scramble the eggs and put it on a separate plate.
2.

Keep the pan heated, add in the green onions and when cooked put in the rice and mix thoroughly. Whisk in the salmon and scrambled eggs accordingly and toss evenly.

3.

While stirring, add the white pepper, freshly ground black pepper, soy sauce and salt. Taste and serve instantly.

9) Stir Fry With Crab Meat

Prep Time: 5 minutes
Cook Time: 15 minutes
Ready In: 20 minutes
Servings: 4

INGREDIENTS:

6 cups cooked rice
1 cup crab meat
1 teaspoon ground white pepper
1 1/2 tablespoons fish sauce
3-5 tablespoons cooking oil
2-3 chopped green onion
3 cloves chopped garlic
2 eggs

DIRECTIONS:

1.
Stir-fry the garlic until fragrant; add in the rice and toss. Put in the crab meat and mix thoroughly.
2.
Crack the eggs and mix it with the fried rice and toss it until evenly mixed. Add in the fish sauce and ground white pepper. Taste and serve with green onions on top.

10) Stir Fry With Walnuts

Prep Time: 40 minutes
Cook Time: 20 minutes
Ready In: 1 hour
Servings: 2

INGREDIENTS:

2 cups cold, cooked white rice
6 walnuts, chopped
½ cup orange segments
2 eggs, beaten
½ pound peeled and deveined medium shrimp
2/3 cup fresh pineapple, diced
2 tablespoons chopped fresh cilantro
2 red onions, sliced
3 green chilli peppers, chopped
1 (1 inch) piece fresh ginger root, minced
1 tablespoon soy sauce
1 tablespoon vegetable oil, divided
Salt and pepper to taste

DIRECTIONS:

1.
In a medium high heat, stir-fry the onions and set aside. Pour in some oil and cook the shrimp for 3 minutes. Set aside.

2.
Cook the ginger until light brown, add in the onion and chilli peppers for a minute. Whisk in the pineapple and oranges. Stir in the rice, walnuts and soy sauce and cook for a few minutes until the rice is hot. Blend in the egg, cilantro and shrimp.
3.
Season with salt and pepper and serve immediately.

11) Stir Fry With Grilled Chicken

Prep Time: 15 minutes
Cook Time: 12 minutes
Ready In: 27 minutes
Servings: 4

INGREDIENTS:

Fried Rice
4 cups Cooked 1 day old rice
Salt and pepper
1 Egg, beaten

For the Gravy
2/3 cup Grilled chicken or duck (chopped)
2/3 cup Shiitake mushroom, diced
1 tsp White pepper powder
1 cup Tomatoes, diced
1/2 cup Carrot, diced
1 tbsp Oyster sauce
2 tbsp Cooking wine
2 tbsp soy sauce
1 tsp Sesame oil
12 small shrimp
1 tbsp Sugar
2 cup Stock
Corn starch

DIRECTIONS:

1.
Scramble the eggs until almost heated; add the rice and mix thoroughly until evenly cooked. Set aside.

2.
For the gravy, sauté the chicken/duck, shrimp, shiitake mushroom and carrots for at least 2 minutes. Put in the stock and wait until it boils. Add the oyster sauce, sugar, soy sauce, tomatoes and cooking wine and stir. When it boils, add sesame oil, white pepper powder for the flavoring. Put some cornstarch to set the sauce.

3.
In a bowl, serve the fried rice with the gravy on top.

12) Stir Fry With Ground Pork

Prep Time: 10 minutes
Cook Time: 5 minutes
Ready In: 15 minutes
Servings: 4
INGREDIENTS:

2 cups cooked white rice (about 3/4 cup uncooked rice)
1 bunch scallions, white and green parts separated and thinly sliced
1/2 pound ground pork
1 tablespoon minced peeled fresh ginger
2 tablespoons plus 1/4 teaspoon soy sauce
2 carrots, shredded
2 eggs, lightly beaten
1 garlic clove, minced
1/2 cup frozen peas
2 tablespoons rice vinegar
2 tablespoons vegetable oil

DIRECTIONS:

1.
Beat the eggs and add soy sauce. Fry the egg without stirring for 1 minute and when cooked, slice it in strips. Set aside.
2.
Fry garlic, scallion white and ginger until fragrant. Combine the pork and cook for 3 minutes

then add the peas, carrots and rice and toss thoroughly. Fold in the cooked egg; add the vinegar and soy sauce and stir evenly until ready. Serve it with scallions green on top.

13) Stir Fry With Bacon

Prep Time: 5 minutes
Cook Time: 7 minutes
Ready In: 12 minutes
Servings: 2

INGREDIENTS:

250g cooked basmati rice
2 rashers bacon, chopped
175g mushrooms, sliced
small knob of fresh root ginger, grated
2 tsp dark soy sauce, plus extra to serve
1 garlic clove, crushed
1 egg, beaten
200g frozen peas
1 tsp sugar
2 tsp oil

DIRECTIONS:

1.
In a heated pan, pour in oil and fry the beaten eggs for 30 seconds. Add the bacon and mushroom and cook until turn to opaque. Put in the garlic, peas and ginger and wait for 1 minute.
2.

Combine sugar and soy sauce. Fry the cooked rice until heated through then whisk the sweetened soy sauce. Put in the egg mixture and serve while its hot.

14)Stir Fry With Chicken Hotdog

Prep Time: 15 minutes
Cook Time: 5 minutes
Ready In: 20 minutes
Servings: 2-4

INGREDIENTS:

3 cups leftover rice
2 pieces medium chicken hotdog (cut diagonally)
3 pieces ham (sweet or salty) cut into strips
1/4 cup mix vegetables(carrot cubes, corn, and green peas)
1 small onions chopped thinly
3 cloves garlic (minced)
1 tablespoon oil
2 stem spring onions
1 teaspoon liquid seasoning (optional)
1/8 teaspoon msg.
1/4 teaspoon salt
2 pieces egg beaten

DIRECTIONS:

1.
Stir fry the garlic until it turns to brown then add the chicken hotdog and ham and cook for 2 minutes.
2.

Fold in the rice, mix vegetables, beaten eggs and stir well until cooked. Add salt, msg, and liquid seasoning for seasoning. Serve and top with spring onions.

15) Stir Fry With Shredded Meat

Prep Time: 15 minutes
Cook Time: 12 minutes
Ready In: 27 minutes
Servings: 4-6

INGREDIENTS:

4 cups cold cooked long-grain rice, white or jasmine rice, grains separated
1/3 cup plain vegetable oil, like soy, corn, or peanut
1/3 pound black forest ham, diced, or about 2 cups cooked, cubed or shredded meat
2-inch piece fresh ginger, peeled and finely chopped
3 whole scallions, thinly sliced on the bias, white and green separated
1 1/3 cups (6 ounces) medley frozen corn, peas, carrots
3 cloves garlic, finely chopped
4 large eggs, lightly beaten
1 onion, diced
Salt and pepper

DIRECTIONS:

1.
Cook the ham until light brown; whisk the onions, salt and pepper and cook for 1-2 minutes. Combine the garlic, scallion whites and ginger and fry for at least 30

seconds. Add also the frozen vegetables until the ice melted and monitor to keep the crunchiness. Set aside.

2.
Scramble the eggs; whisk some salt pepper to taste. Set aside. Stir-fry the rice until reached the desired crispiness. Add the scallion.

3.
In a large bowl, toss the fried rice, scrambled eggs and the ham mixture together, add some seasoning to taste and serve.

16) Stir Fry With Tomato Sauce

Prep Time: 10 minutes
Cook Time: 10 minutes
Ready In: 20 minutes
Servings: 2

INGREDIENTS:

Cooked basmati rice- 4 cups
Tomato sauce-1 tbsp
Vegetables- chopped(use carrots,beans&cabbage)-2 cups
Ginger and garlic -chopped finely- 1 tbsp
Green chili - finely chopped-1
Spring onion chopped-2 tbsp
Black pepper powder- to taste
Celery chopped-3 to 4 tbsp
Onion -chopped- 1 small
Soya sauce-1 tbsp
White vinegar-1/4 tsp
Salt to taste
Oil

DIRECTIONS:

1.
Mix tomato sauce, soya sauce and vinegar in a separate bowl. Set aside.
2.

Sauté garlic, green chillies and ginger until fragrant. Add the onion and cook until it becomes transparent. Put in the spring onion, chopped vegetables and celery and cook for a minute or two. Add the cooked rice and blend the tomato sauce mixture; toss thoroughly. Serve while it is hot.

17) Stir Fry With Cauliflower

Prep Time: 10 minutes
Cook Time: 5 minutes
Ready In: 15 minutes
Servings: 1

INGREDIENTS:

1 cup cauliflower, grated
1 large egg
¼ cup chopped scallions
2 tablespoons soy sauce
2 teaspoons garlic
1 tablespoon extra-virgin olive oil

DIRECTIONS:

1.
Use cauliflower instead of rice. Grate cauliflower into bits or place it in a food processor until almost similar to the size of rice.
2.
In a medium high pan, cook the onion and garlic until fragrant. Put in the cauliflower and cook for 4-5 minutes, be careful not to overcook it. Add soy sauce then put in the beaten eggs; toss evenly.
3.
Whisk in the green onion tops and serve.

18) Stir Fry With Mushrooms And Carrots

Prep Time: 20 minutes
Cook Time: 10 hour
Ready In: 30 minutes
Servings: 3-4

INGREDIENTS:

    FRIED RICE
3 cups cooked brown rice, cooled
About 8 ounces shiitake mushrooms (or a mix of mushrooms), wiped clean and sliced
1 large carrot cut in a half inch dice
1/2 cup chopped cashews, plus a few whole cashews for garnish
2 tablespoons canola, vegetable, or other neutral oil
4 scallions, white and light green parts, chopped
1 tablespoon minced, peeled fresh ginger
3 eggs, beaten with a 1/4 teaspoon salt
4 cloves garlic, minced
1 tablespoon soy sauce
1 yellow onion, diced
Salt

DIRECTIONS:

1.
Fry the mushroom until fragrant then put in the garlic and season with salt; cook for 1 minute. Set aside.

2.
Cook the onion, carrots and scallions into a heated pan for 1-2 minutes. Whisk in the garlic and ginger, wait until fragrant. Stir in the rice and mix well and wait until it becomes a bit crispy. Season with soy sauce then add the mushroom.

3.
Move the fried rice into the half of the pan, add some oil them scramble the eggs. When the scramble eggs are fully cooked, toss it with the fried rice thoroughly. Pour in the cashews and toss. Best if served with minted fruit salad on the side.

19) Stir Fry With Cabbage

Prep Time: 15 minutes
Cook Time: 15 minutes
Ready In: 30 minutes
Servings: 6

INGREDIENTS:

3 cups leftover cooked Rice
OR 1 cup uncooked Rice with 1 Tbsp butter and 1/2 tsp salt
1 small or 1/2 large green cabbage, (about 8 cups), finely sliced
1/8 tsp freshly ground black pepper, or to taste
1 tsp sesame oil (you'll be glad you used it)
1 large carrot (1 cup) peeled and grated
1 medium onion (1 cup), finely diced
1/4 tsp salt (or to taste or no salt at all)
2 Tbsp cooking oil
2 Tbsp unsalted butter
2 Tbsp Soy Sauce

DIRECTIONS:

1.
Cook the rice according to the package instruction with ½ tsp. salt and 1 tbsp butter. When ready, set aside.
2.

Sauté the cabbage, onion and carrrot with 2 tbsp cooking oil and wait until the cabbage is wilted. Stir frequently. Fold in cooked rice and add some butter and toss evenly. For the taste, season it with soy sauce, sesame oil, salt and pepper. Serve while it is hot.

20) Stir Fry With Raisins

Prep Time: 15 minutes
Cook Time: 30 minutes
Ready In: 1 hour 45 minutes
Servings: 4

INGREDIENTS:

1 cup uncooked jasmine rice
1 teaspoon raisins
½ cup water
5 canned lychees, drained and quartered
3 tablespoons soy based liquid seasoning
¼ cup reduced-sodium soy sauce
3 tablespoons vegetable oil
1 tablespoon chopped cashews
2 cloves garlic, minced
¼ teaspoon white sugar
2 tablespoons chopped green onion
2 tablespoons chopped carrot
1 tablespoon chopped onion
14 teaspoon white pepper

DIRECTIONS:

1.
Cook the rice for 20-25 minutes; when ready transfer it to a plate, spread and refrigerate for a while.

2.
Stir-fry the garlic and cook until fragrant. Add in the carrots and onion mix well until cooked. Fold in the cooked rice and toss evenly. Whisk in the raisins, cashews, soy sauce, soy seasoning, green onions, salt and white pepper. Cook and toss until heated through. Top it with the quartered lychees and serve.

21) Stir Fry With Corn

Prep Time: 15 minutes
Cook Time: 15 minutes
Ready In: 30 minutes
Servings: 3

INGREDIENTS:

1 cup Basmati rice
10-12 beans (baby beans)
1 tsp pepper (white preffered)
3-4 sprig spring onion
5-6 Baby corn
3 tbsp olive oil
½ tsp sugar
1 carrot

DIRECTION:

1.
Cook rice with 1 ½ cup water and when ready refrigerate it for a while.
2.
In a heated pan, put some oil and combine the beans, baby corn and carrots; toss and whisk some sugar then sauté for 2 minutes. Add in the spring onion and pepper and cook for a minute. Fold in the cooked rice and toss until heated through. Serve while it is hot.

22) Stir Fry With Capsicum

Prep Time: 15 minutes
Cook Time: 30 minutes
Ready In: 45 minutes
Servings: 4

INGREDIENTS:

2 cups Chinese rice
1/2 cup shredded capsicum
1/2 cup French beans, cut diagonally into thin strips
1/2 cup carrot, cut into long thin strips
1 cup chopped spring onions whites
1 cup chopped spring onion greens
1 tbsp chopped celery
1 tsp soy sauce
Salt to taste
1 tbsp oil

DIRECTIONS:

1.
In a heated pan, cook the vegetables, spring onions whites and celery for 3-4 minutes.
2.
Put in the rice, spring onion greens and season with soya sauce and salt. Toss thoroughly for 2-3 minutes and serve.

23) Stir Fry With Fried Cashews

Prep Time: 5 minutes
Cook Time: 15 minutes
Ready In: 20 minutes
Servings: 4

INGREDIENTS:

1 cup leftover white rice
fried cashews
2 tablespoons spring onions
2 tablespoons fried chicken, diced (of your choice) or 2 tablespoons assorted fresh vegetables, chopped (of your choice)
2 tablespoons pineapple, chopped
2 teaspoons raisins
1/2 teaspoon white pepper powder
1/4 teaspoon sugar
1 teaspoon soy sauce
1 teaspoon salt
1 teaspoon oil
1 teaspoon garlic, chopped
2 eggs, whisked

DIRECTIONS:

1.

Stir-fry the garlic until fragrant. Add in the rice, eggs, chicken, vegetables, spring onions and season with salt, soy sauce, sugar and white pepper powder. Toss evenly.

2.

Put in the raisins and pineapples and mix well. Serve it with fried cashews on top.

24) Stir Fry With Coriander Seed And Mango

Prep Time: 10 minutes
Cook Time: 20 minutes
Ready In: 30 minutes
Servings: 4-6

INGREDIENTS:

6 cups cold jasmine rice
2 teaspoons crushed coriander seed
2 mangos, peeled, sliced into 1/2 inch pieces (about 1 1/2 cups)
3/4 cup roasted cashews
3 tablespoons tamari or soy sauce (tamari is gluten free, soy sauce is not)
6 oz green beans (about 1 1/2 cups)
tablespoons peanut or 15 basil leaves, chiffonade
1 medium red onion, diced medium
1 tablespoon fresh minced ginger
1/4 teaspoon red pepper flakes
2 tablespoons fresh lime juice
1 tablespoon Sriracha hot sauce
1 tomato, cut into 1/2 inch pieces
canola oil, divided
3 cloves garlic, minced
Fresh cilantro

DIRECTIONS:

1.
In a heated pan, for 3-5 minutes cook the green beans with oil and whisk some salt and set aside.

2.
Stir-fry the onions until it turned transparent, add in the coriander, garlic, ginger, red pepper flakes and toss for 30 seconds. Put in the cold rice and mix well.

3.
Fold in the tamari, tomato and hot sauce, mix well and cook for 3 minutes until the rice turned to brown. Add in the mangoes, string beans, cashews, basil leaves and lime juice. Cook for a minute or two then put some salt for the taste. Scatter cilantro on top and serve.

25) Stir Fry With Apricots

Prep Time: 15 minutes
Cook Time: 30 minutes
Ready In: 45 minutes
Servings: 4

INGREDIENTS:

1 1/2 cups basmati rice, rinsed and drained
1/2 cup diced dried apricots
2 large eggs, lightly beaten together in a small bowl
4 scallions, green parts only, chopped into 1/4-inch lengths
2 tablespoons finely chopped shallots (from 1 to 2 shallots)
1 tablespoon finely chopped garlic (from about 2 garlic cloves)
2 tablespoons chopped fresh parsley (chives or cilantro also work)
freshly ground black pepper
1/4 cup sliced almonds, toasted
3 tablespoons vegetable oil
pinch of saffron threads
1 teaspoon kosher salt
1/4 cup half-and-half

DIRECTIONS:

1.

Cook in a microwave the mixed milk and saffron for 30 minutes and set aside.

2.

In a pan, fry the apricots, shallot and garlic for 1 minute. Mix the rice and some salt cook until heated through. Pour in the milk mixture and bring to a boil. Cover the pan, and wait for 10-12 minutes until the rice absorbed the milk. Set aside.

3.

Scramble the eggs in a large skillet and whirl to cover the bottom. Stir frequently until it turns into small bits for 1 minute. Put in the scallions, mix and cook for another 1 minute. Combine the rice mixture until evenly mixed. Put seasonings and top it with toasted almonds and parsley and serve.

26) Plain Stir Fry

Prep Time: 5 minutes
Cook Time: 5 minutes
Ready In: 10 minutes
Servings: 4-6

INGREDIENTS:

4 cups cold cooked rice
1 - 2 green onions, as desired
2 large eggs
1 - 2 tablespoons light soy sauce or oyster sauce, as desired
4 tablespoons oil for stir-frying, or as needed
1 teaspoon salt
Pepper to taste

DIRECTIONS:

1.
In a frying pan, scramble the eggs but avoid cooking it too dry. Set aside.
2.
Stir-fry the rice until it reached its crispiness. Add the scrambled eggs and toss thoroughly. Serve it with green onions on top.

27) Stir Fry With Shallots

Prep Time: 5 minutes
Cook Time: 5 minutes
Ready In: 10 minutes
Servings: 2

INGREDIENTS:

2 servings cooked rice (about 200g), refrigerated overnight
5 cloves of garlic, minced
3 shallots, minced
1 egg, beaten, seasoned with 1 tsp of light soy sauce
spring onions, chopped
2 tbsp cooking oil
salt, to taste

DIRECTIONS:

1.
Cook the shallots and garlic with oil and wait until fragrant. Mix in the cooked rice and toss thoroughly.
2.
Put the beaten eggs with the rice; mix well until crispy. Add seasoning to taste and transfer it to a plate and scatter chopped spring onions on top. Serve.

28) Stir Fry With Ginger

Prep Time: 10 minutes
Cook Time: 20 minutes
Ready In: 30 minutes
Servings: 4

INGREDIENTS:

2/3 cup raw instant rice
1 teaspoon finely chopped fresh ginger
4 spring onions, finely chopped
1 tablespoon (15ml) sesame oil
2 eggs, beaten
soy sauce to taste

DIRECTIONS:

1.
Cook the raw rice according to the package instruction. Let it cool down for a while. Stir fry the cooked rice and add soy sauce to taste. Toss frequently until light brown. Set Aside.
2.
Scramble the eggs and put in the fried rice. Mix in the spring onions and ginger until combined evenly and serve.

29) Stir Fry With Broccoli

Prep Time: 5 minutes
Cook Time: 10 minutes
Ready In: 15 minutes
Servings: 2

INGREDIENTS:

4 cups very cold cooked brown rice
1 cup peeled, finely diced broccoli stems (from about 1-1/4 lb. broccoli)
2 Tbs. finely grated fresh ginger
3/4 cup finely diced red bell pepper
4 scallions (both white and green parts), thinly sliced
3/4 cup finely diced Canadian bacon (4 oz.)
3/4 cup frozen shelled edamame
3/4 cup corn kernels, fresh or frozen
2 large cloves garlic, minced
3/4 cup finely diced carrots
2 large eggs, lightly beaten
1/4 cup lower-sodium soy sauce
2 Tbs. canola oil

DIRECTIONS:

1.
In a large wok, pour some oil and put in the broccoli stems, carrots and bell pepper. Sauté for 3-5 minutes until reached the desired softness of vegetables.

2.
Add the corn and edamame until the latter is melted. Put in the garlic, scallion and ginger, stir until fragrant. Mix in the rice and bacon; toss frequently for 3-5 minutes.

3.
Set the fried rice in the half side of the wok; scramble the eggs. Mix and stir evenly the fried rice and the scrambled eggs. Whisk in soy sauce to taste and serve.

30) Stir Fry With Mozzarella Cheese And Ketchup

Prep Time: 15 minutes
Cook Time: 0 minutes
Ready In: 1 hour 15 minutes
Servings: 4

INGREDIENTS:

Cooked rice, 100g
Mozzarella cheese, a few
Ketchup, 1 tbsp
Broccoli, 50g, boiled
Cashew nut, 10g
Ham, 50g

Shrimp, 50g
Corn, 30g
Raisin, 10g
Egg, 2pc
Salt and black pepper to taste

DIRECTIONS:

1.

In a medium heated pan, fry the eggs to make an omelette and set aside. Using the same pan, lightly fry the shrimp.

2.

Stir-fry the rice, corn, ham and shrimp; add in the ketchup and toss. Toss the raisins and the mix cashew nuts.

3.

Serve the omelette on top of fried rice. Garnish it with the mozzarella cheese; broccoli and ketchup.

31) Stir Fry With Cherry Tomatoes

Prep Time: 10 minutes
Cook Time: 20 minutes
Ready In: 30 minutes
Servings: 4

INGREDIENTS:

4 cups cooked brown rice (11/3 cups dry rice)
cherry tomatoes, halved, coriander leaves, to serve
2 rashers shortcut rindless bacon, finely chopped
1 red capsicum, seeded, finely chopped
1 green capsicum, seeded, finely chopped
125g can corn kernels, drained
6 green onions, thinly sliced
¼ cup light soy sauce
¼ cup hoisin sauce
1 tablespoon sesame oil
1 onion, finely chopped

DIRECTIONS:

1.
For 3-4 minutes, sauté the bacon, capsicum and onion. Combine rice, onion, corn and sauces. Mix well and cook for 2-3 minutes. Set aside.
2.

Put in a sealed or box container, top it with cherry tomatoes and coriander leaves. Refrigerate for a while and serve.

Cauliflower Chicken Fried Rice

Serving: 4 | Prep: 30mins | Cook: 14mins | Ready in:

Ingredients

3/4 pound skinless, boneless chicken breasts, cut into small cubes

6 tablespoons soy sauce, divided

1 tablespoon brown sugar

2 teaspoons sesame oil, divided

1 teaspoon cornstarch

3 tablespoons vegetable oil

5 scallions, chopped, light and dark green parts separated

4 garlic cloves, minced

1 (1 1/2 inch) piece fresh ginger, grated

2 pounds cauliflower rice

1 teaspoon kosher salt, divided

1 1/2 cups frozen peas and carrots

2 eggs, beaten

1/2 cup finely diced fresh pineapple

1/4 cup chopped peanuts (optional)

1 tablespoon rice vinegar

Direction

In a large bowl, combine together cornstarch, 1 teaspoon of sesame oil, brown sugar, 1 tablespoon of soy sauce and chicken.

Heat a large saucepan or a wok on high heat. Swirl in 1 tablespoon of vegetable oil. Spread the chicken mixture over the wok's surface in a single layer; cook for 1 minute. Turn over; toss the chicken. Spread out again; cook while stirring for 2 more minutes. Move the chicken onto a plate.

Place the wok on medium heat and heat the remaining 2 tablespoons of vegetable oil. Put in ginger, garlic and the light green part of the scallions; cook while stirring for 1-2 minute, till soften and fragrant.

Mix in 1/2 teaspoon of salt, cauliflower rice and 4 tablespoons of soy sauce. Cook for around 3 minutes, till the cauliflower begins to crisp. Mix in carrots and peas. Cook while stirring occasionally for around 5 minutes, till warm through.

In the center of the wok, form a well; transfer in beaten eggs. Using a spatula, mix eggs for 2 minutes, till scrambled. Mix in rice vinegar, peanuts, pineapple, the dark green parts of the scallions, the remaining 1 teaspoon of sesame oil, the remaining 1 tablespoon of soy sauce and chicken.

Nutrition Information

Calories: 389 calories;

Total Carbohydrate: 25

Cholesterol: 137

Protein: 28.5

Total Fat: 21.3

Sodium: 1977

Cheesy Chicken Stir Fry

Serving: 6 | Prep: 10mins | Cook: 30mins | Ready in:
Ingredients
2 cups uncooked white rice
4 cups water
1 tablespoon olive oil
1 teaspoon garlic salt
1 teaspoon black pepper
1 teaspoon dried parsley
3 skinless, boneless chicken breast halves, cut into strips
2 cups chopped broccoli
1 cup sliced carrots
1 cup sugar snap peas
1 (10.75 ounce) can condensed cheddar cheese soup, such as Campbell's®
1/2 cup shredded Cheddar cheese
Direction
In saucepan, boil water and rice on high heat. Lower heat to moderately-low, put on cover, and let simmer for 20 to 25 minutes till rice is soft and liquid has been

soaked in. Rest rice with cover while you complete the rest of the steps.

In a wok or big skillet, heat parsley, black pepper, garlic salt and olive oil on moderate heat.

In olive oil, cook and mix the strips of chicken for 5 to 7 minutes till juices run clear and not pink anymore in the middle.

Mix in snap peas, carrots and broccoli; place skillet cover, and cook for 5 to 8 minutes, till carrots are soft. Into the vegetables and chicken, mix condensed Cheddar cheese soup; combine thoroughly and simmer. Cook and mix till vegetables and chicken are covered in sauce.

To serve, on platter, pile cooked rice, and put vegetables and chicken in sauce on top. Scatter shredded Cheddar cheese on top and serve.

Nutrition Information

Calories: 425 calories;

Cholesterol: 44

Protein: 21.2

Total Fat: 9.4

Sodium: 786

Total Carbohydrate: 61.2

Chef John's Caramel Chicken

Serving: 4 | Prep: 20mins | Cook: 20mins | Ready in:

Ingredients

3/4 cup dark brown sugar

1/3 cup cold water

1/3 cup fish sauce

1/3 cup rice vinegar

1 tablespoon soy sauce

4 cloves garlic, crushed

1 tablespoon fresh grated ginger

1 teaspoon vegetable oil

8 boneless, skinless chicken thighs, quartered

1/2 cup roasted peanuts

2 fresh jalapeno peppers, seeded and sliced

1 bunch green onions, chopped

fresh cilantro sprigs, for garnish

Direction

In a bowl, whisk water, brown sugar, rice vinegar, fish sauce, ginger, garlic, and soy sauce together for about 1 minute till brown sugar is dissolved completely. Leave aside.

In a skillet, heat oil over high heat. Mix in the chicken.

Pour 1/3 cup of the brown sugar mixture over chicken; cook and stir for around 6 to 7 minutes till the brown sugar mixture has a syrup-like consistency.

Pour in the rest of brown sugar mixture; cook for 5 minutes till chicken is no longer pink inside and tender.

Mix in green onion, jalapenos and peanuts; cook for around 2 to 3 minutes till warmed through.

Add cilantro for garnishing and serve.

Nutrition Information

Calories: 615 calories;

Total Fat: 33.2

Sodium: 1967

Total Carbohydrate: 37.9

Cholesterol: 129

Protein: 43

Chef John's Cashew Chicken

Serving: 2 | Prep: 20mins | Cook: 10mins | Ready in:
Ingredients
2 grilled skinless, boneless chicken breasts, cut into 1-inch pieces
1 pinch salt and ground black pepper to taste
1 tablespoon cornstarch

1/2 cup cold water
1 lemon, juiced
1 1/2 tablespoons rice vinegar
1 tablespoon ketchup
1 tablespoon soy sauce, or more to taste
1 tablespoon packed brown sugar
2 teaspoons Asian chile pepper sauce (such as sambal oelek)
2 tablespoons vegetable oil
1 fresh hot red chile pepper, sliced
6 thin slices fresh ginger root
1/2 cup dry-roasted cashews
2 cloves garlic, sliced
1/4 cup chopped cilantro

Direction

Use black pepper and salt to season the chicken cubes. In a bowl, combine water and cornstarch until the mixture is smooth; whip in chile pepper sauce, brown sugar, soy sauce, ketchup, rice vinegar and lemon juice, stirring until the cornstarch is lump-free and brown sugar has dissolved.

Put a heavy skillet on medium-high heat; add vegetable oil. Put ginger and red chili slices into hot oil. Cook while stirring constantly until the oil is flavored, approximately 2 minutes. Stir in garlic and cashews; cook until the cashews turn golden brown lightly, approximately 2 more minutes.

Toss cashew mixture and seasoned chicken cubes in the skillet gently until blended, approximately half a minute. Reduce the heat to medium-low and add cornstarch mixture. Stir often until the sauce has thickened, approximately half a minute. Pour in a splash of water if the sauce is too thick. Simmer for another 2 minutes so that the chicken is thoroughly heated. Modify the amount of chile pepper sauce, soy sauce, black pepper and salt to taste. Put in cilantro and stir just until it wilts, approximately 15 seconds.

Nutrition Information
Calories: 539 calories;
Total Fat: 32.9
Sodium: 829
Total Carbohydrate: 30.4
Cholesterol: 73
Protein: 33.5

Chettinad Style Chicken

Serving: 6 | Prep: 15mins | Cook: 45mins | Ready in:
Ingredients
2 1/4 pounds skinless, boneless chicken breast, cut into bite-sized chunks
1 teaspoon turmeric
salt to taste
1/4 cup vegetable oil
2 teaspoons poppy seeds
2 teaspoons whole black peppercorns
2 teaspoons fennel seed
2 teaspoons coriander seed

1 teaspoon cumin seed
3 large onions, minced
4 green chile peppers, chopped
2 sprigs fresh curry leaves
1 tablespoon ginger paste
1 teaspoon garlic paste
1 cup chopped fresh tomatoes
1/2 cup water

Direction

Rub salt and turmeric on chicken pieces; put aside. Heat oil in big skillet/kadhai on medium heat; fry cumin seed, coriander seed, fennel seed, peppercorns and poppy seeds in hot oil till they just start to change color. Take out of the skillet, keeping oil in skillet. Use mortar and pestle to grind spice mixture; put aside. Add garlic paste, ginger paste, curry leaves, green chile peppers and onion to leftover oil; cook for 7-10 minutes till onions are golden brown. Mix ground spices and tomatoes into mixture; cook till tomatoes are soft. Add chicken; season with salt. Simmer for 5 minutes. Put water on mixture and cover; cook for 30 minutes till chicken is not pink in center anymore and juices are clear. Serve hot.

Nutrition Information
Calories: 358 calories;
Total Fat: 15.4
Sodium: 128
Total Carbohydrate: 13.5
Cholesterol: 104
Protein: 40.5

Chicken 'n' Peppers

Serving: 6 servings. | Prep: 10mins | Cook: 15mins | Ready in:

Ingredients

3/4 cup chicken broth
1/4 cup soy sauce
2 garlic cloves, minced
2 tablespoons cornstarch
3/4 teaspoon ground ginger
1/4 teaspoon cayenne pepper
6 boneless skinless chicken breast halves (4 ounces each), cut into 1-inch pieces
1 tablespoon canola oil
1 each medium green, yellow and sweet red peppers, cut into 1-inch pieces
1/4 cup water

Direction

Mix together cayenne pepper, ginger, cornstarch, garlic, soy sauce and broth in a big bowl. Put in chicken and stir to coat well. In a big skillet, heat oil on medium high heat. Put in chicken mixture. Bring to a boil, then cook and stir until thickened, or about 2 minutes.
Lower to medium heat. Put in water and peppers then cook and stir until peppers are softened, or about 5 to 8 minutes.
Nutrition Information

Calories: 200 calories

Fiber: 0 fiber)

Total Carbohydrate: 8g carbohydrate (0 sugars

Cholesterol: 73mg cholesterol

Protein: 29g protein. Diabetic Exchanges: 3 lean meat

Total Fat: 7g fat (0 saturated fat)

Sodium: 207mg sodium

Chicken Apricot Stir Fry

Serving: 2 serving. | Prep: 5mins | Cook: 15mins | Ready in:

Ingredients

1/2 pound boneless skinless chicken breasts, cut into strips
1 teaspoon canola oil
1 cup fresh snow peas
6 tablespoons apricot preserves
1/4 cup water
1 garlic clove, minced
1-1/2 teaspoons sesame oil
1 teaspoon sesame seeds, toasted
1 teaspoon reduced-sodium soy sauce
1/4 teaspoon ground ginger
1/4 teaspoon Dijon mustard
Hot cooked rice

Direction

Stir-fry chicken with canola oil in a wok or big skillet about 3 minutes. Put in mustard, ginger, soy sauce, sesame seeds, sesame oil, garlic, water, preserves and snow peas. Bring the mixture to a boil. Lower heat and simmer without a cover until vegetables are softened and chicken is not pink anymore, about 5 to 7 minutes. Serve together with rice.

Nutrition Information

Calories: 364 calories

Total Carbohydrate: 46g carbohydrate (25g sugars

Cholesterol: 63mg cholesterol

Protein: 26g protein.

Total Fat: 9g fat (2g saturated fat)

Sodium: 258mg sodium

Fiber: 3g fiber)

www.ingramcontent.com/pod-product-compliance
Lightning Source LLC
Chambersburg PA
CBHW071441070526
44578CB00001B/179